THE

78TH DIVISION

IN THE

FINAL - OFFENSIVE

IN

ITALY

The Naval & Military Press Ltd

Published by

The Naval & Military Press Ltd
Unit 5 Riverside, Brambleside
Bellbrook Industrial Estate
Uckfield, East Sussex
TN22 1QQ England

Tel: +44 (0)1825 749494

www.naval-military-press.com
www.nmarchive.com

In reprinting in facsimile from the original, any imperfections are inevitably reproduced and the quality may fall short of modern type and cartographic standards.

THE 78th DIVISION IN THE FINAL OFFENSIVE IN ITALY

An account of the operations of the 78th Infantry Division during the period 9th to 25th April 1945

PART I: Connecting Narrative

CONTENTS

1.	Introduction.	page 1
Chapter 1.	The 5th Corps attack across the rivers Senio and Santerno.	page 1
Chapter 2.	Preliminary operations of the 78th Division.	page 2
Chapter 3.	Composition of the 78th Division.	page 6
Chapter 4.	The break-out from the Santerno bridgehead.	page 8
Chapter 5.	The breaking of the Argenta Gap.	page 14
Chapter 6.	The advance to the Po di Volano.	page 20
Chapter 7.	Destruction of the enemy south of the river Po.	page 25
Table 1.	Casualty figures for 78 Division 9 — 25 April.	page 29
Table 2.	Prisoners of War taken by 78 Division 9 — 25 April.	page 36

PART II: Unit Accounts.

CONTENTS

Chapter 1.	11 Brigade Headquarters.	page 38
Chapter 2.	5th Battalion The Northamptonshire Regiment.	page 41
Chapter 3.	1st Battalion The East Surrey Regiment.	page 43
Chapter 4.	2nd Battalion The Lancashire Fusiliers.	page 47
Chapter 5.	5th Battalion The Buffs.	page 50
Chapter 6.	8th Argyll and Sutherland Highlanders	page 54
Chapter 7.	38 (Irish) Infantry Brigade.	page 56
Chapter 8.	2nd Battalion The Royal Inniskilling Fusiliers.	page 60
Chapter 9.	2nd Battalion The London Irish Rifles.	page 63
Chapter 10.	Supporting Arms.	page 69

MAPS. (See end of Part II).

Plate 1.	The situation at 1200 hrs 9 Apr 45. Scale 1 : 250,000.
Plate 2.	The situation at 1800 hrs 10 Apr 45. Scale 1 : 50,000.
Plate 3.	The concentration around Lugo on 11 Apr 45. Scale 1 : 50,000.
Plate 4.	The advance from the Santerno to the Reno. Scale 1 : 50,000.
Plate 5.	The breaking of the Argenta Gap. Scale 1 : 50,000.
Plate 6.	The advance from the Argenta Gap to the Po di Volano. Scale 1 : 50,000.
Plate 7.	Closing on the river Po. Scale 1 : 50,000.
Plate 8.	The advance from the Senio to the Po. Scale 1 : 250,000.

PART ONE

Introduction.

The 15th Army Group, consisting of the Fifth and Eighth Armies, landed in Italy in September 1943. Fifteen months later, in December 1944, after long and bitter warfare up the whole straggling length of the country, after crossing innumerable rivers and forcing the passes in the mountains, after breaking successively each of the enemy's natural lines of defence, a total gain of some 600 miles had been achieved and the front line of the Eighth Army was formed along the river Senio in the plain of Lombardy.

From January to April the two Armies were engaged in a static warfare as close and intense as that in which the two sides remained locked from 1914 to 1918; stalemate had been reached.

By the beginning of April 1945 weather conditions had improved sufficiently to allow the Allied offensive to be resumed.

The main offensive of the 15th Army Group began at 1920 hrs on April 9th when the Eighth Army, supported by strong air forces, attacked and broke the enemy's line on the river Senio.

The punch of this attack was delivered by the 5th Corps, assaulting with the 8th Indian Division on the right and the 2nd New Zealand Division on the left. 56 Div were given the role of executing important subsidiary ops in the coastal area.

Between these two first mentioned divisions a sector of the river-line was held by the 78th Infantry Division with the 2nd Armoured Brigade less one regiment under its command.

CHAPTER I.

The 5th Corps Attack Across the Rivers Senio and Santerno.

April 9th dawned fine and warm by the banks of the Senio, with the ground hard underfoot and a cloudless sky. It was ideal weather for the air forces to begin that process ominously known as "softening-up".

The morning passed in comparative peace except at each headquarters, where telephones rang incessantly and paper continued to pour from the machinery of planning and fall into every lap "for action" or "for information"; liaison officers came and went, and generally came again: on the river bank it was unusually quiet.

At 1350 hours the first rumblings of attack began with medium and heavy bombers passing overhead on their way to drop a "carpet" of small fragmentation bombs in the enemy's rear areas. Ten minutes later the first "cabrank" appeared; Spitfires circling high up in the sky, ready to pounce on targets chosen by the ground forces.

At 1520 hours the overture began in earnest; first guns and mortars, then the air, then guns again, then both; there was no mistaking this, the prelude of assault.

The bombardment was planned and carried out in five phases. Each phase opened with an intense gun-attack, employing every available gun and mortar on the Corps front. Then followed a ten-minute period during which the guns were silent and fighter-bombers strafed the river banks with cannon. Next, the aircraft switched to the area behind the river and attacked with bombs, while the guns and mortars also lifted from the floodbank and laid down concentrations beyond it.

This cycle of destruction revolved five times between 1520 and 1920 hours, the time planned for the ground assault, the time known as "H".

The artillery and mortar bombardment for the fifth phase of the attack ended at 1920 hours precisely; the fighter-bombers came down to strafe the river bank; but the attack was a feint. As the aircraft swooped, "Wasp" and "Crocodile" flamethrowers all along the river bank opened their jets and the enemy's posts were subjected to intense saturation of flame on an unprecedented scale. This was the climax of the "preparation".

At "H" the leading infantry assaulted across the river, and the opening barrage began.

For two hours the fog of war lay thickly over the front and conflicting news confounded efforts to paint a military picture with chinagraph on talc. By 2115 hours, however, it was clear that substantial bridgeheads had been gained in the initial assault and progress seemed, on the whole, to be good.

During the night and all next day the Indians on the right and the New Zealanders on the left continued to make steady and substantial progress. By dawn on April 11th they were approaching the second major obstacle in the way of the advance — the Santerno river. By nightfall on the same date the Santerno had been crossed and each of the two leading divisions had a foothold on the far bank. The work of the 78th Division was about to begin.

CHAPTER II.

Preliminary Operations of the 78th Division.

On 'D' day the divisional sector was held by 11 Brigade with under command the Queen's Bays, 5 Buffs, 6 RWK and a composite squadron of 56 Recce Regiment. 5 Northamptons, supported by the 75 mm SP guns of 56 Recce Regiment were detached from the Division filling a gap in the Corps front near Alfonsine. 36 and 38 Brigades, and 2 Armoured Brigade less 10H. were concentrated in rear areas prepared to move forward when required. 10H was detached from its brigade and under command of the 56th (London) Division in the North.

Elsewhere many of the division's supporting arms were engaged in sundry tasks. The entire Divisional Artillery, including 11 RHA, was placed in support of the 2nd New Zealand Division for the preliminary gun attack and subsequently for the assault. By agreement with the New Zealanders, however, 138 Field Regiment was retained with its primary task, the support of the divisional sector.

In order to thicken the gunner support on the Division's front two batteries, each of six tanks equipped with 105 mm guns, were formed from 2 Armoured Brigade, (Bays and 9L), and placed under command 11 RHA.

1 Kensingtons were deployed in support of the flanking divisions, having placed two platoons of heavy mortars with each.

The "Wasp" Flamethrowers of the Division were dispersed along the Corps front so that the moral and physical onslaught which was planned as the climax of the preparation might be most effective on the fronts of the assaulting formations, but that the exact area of attack should remain concealed until the infantry were across.. Nine were placed under command of each of the two assaulting divisions, and nine remained with 11 Brigade in the Divisional sector.

The Divisional Engineers were also engaged on tasks of assistance to the flanks, and in particular on the business of road maintenance.

With the Division thus deployed the preliminary air attacks on D day necessitated the withdrawal of our own troops to a distance of 400 yards from the river bank. This operation was carried out by 11 Brigade at first light on April 9th, in conformity with the flanking divisions.

At H hour previous positions were to be re-occupied and 11 Brigade was then to push forward on the extreme right to occupy positions on the Eastern flood bank some 300 or 400 yards beyond the original line, which here ran that distance short of the river.

In carrying out this task the Brigade encountered some difficulty. By 2010 hours all positions previously held in the Division's sector were re-occupied, but 2 LF. supported by a squadron of Bays, were meeting strong opposition as they tried to move forward to the new positions on the right. Enemy machine-guns were very active from the area of the floodbank, and many mines were causing some trouble. A further impediment came from individual enemy who, having observed our withdrawal early in the day, had moved forward from their posts and thus succeeded in avoiding the main weight of the air attack. These few enterprising huns kept bobbing up in the rear of the LF. With the machine-gunners in the bank they inflicted between 20 and 30 casualties, preventing the battalion from gaining the new position by dusk.

The progress of the main assault during the night of April 9th caused the enemy to withdraw from his positions on the Division's front by dawn on the 10th. When this was discovered 11 Brigade at once crossed the river and occupied the Western bank. By 0940 hours one company of 1 Surreys reached Cotignola without trouble, and here contact was made with 27 New Zealand Battalion which had entered the village from the West. Soon afterwards the New Zealanders moved on and at 1020 hours 11 Brigade was ordered to make firm the general area of the village. At the same time arrangements were made for necessary vehicles, and in particular anti-tank guns, to be passed over a bridge in the New Zealanders' sector and to join 11 Brigade's troops in Cotignola.

While these operations were in progress, and the flanking divisions were pushing rapidly on, the Divisional Engineers were hard at work. As soon as 11 Brigade had crossed the river and occupied the far bank, a sapper recce party had gone forward and made a search for a suitable bridging place. By 1100 hours a site was chosen and work began at once.

At this time all indications pointed to a speedy sweep forward by the Indians and New Zealanders, and it was thought that the Division might be called upon to move up at any time. Once the two leading formations linked up to the West of the little town of Lugo there would be nothing, except the problems of movement, to prevent the Division from concentrating between the Senio and the Santerno. That this should be done as soon as possible was vital to the maintenance of momentum in the whole offensive.

In preparation for this expected move a preliminary concentration of the Division was effected during the day in the wake of 11 Brigade's movements.

36 and 38 Brigades moved, during the early part of the day, to areas South and East of Bagnacavallo and those units of 11 Brigade which were not engaged in occupation of ground to the West of the river concentrated in the Brigade's original sector.

2 Armoured Brigade remained in an area further to the North-East.

The Divisional Artillery moved forward during the morning to positions just short of the Senio, the better thus to support the New Zealanders.

By mid-day much "teeing up" had been done: the "Wasps" and heavy mortar platoons which had been lent to the flanks had returned to their parent units; an officer from the "Flail" Squadron of 51 RTR had visited Divisional Headquarters during the morning and made arrangements to link his squadron to the Division when across the river: in the north 5 Northamptons were beginning to concentrate in preparation for rejoining 11 Brigade; in every quarter planning and recconaissance were in progress and all awaited the signal to move.

In the afternoon the Divisional Commander attended a conference held by the Corps Commander and returned to hold his own at the headquarters of 11 Brigade. The plan had been somewhat changed. Originally it had been the intention that 38 (Irish) Brigade should be passed over the Santerno river into the bridgehead of either the New Zealand or the Indian Division, and that it should thence strike out Northwards or Westwards as might be required. At the same time 36 Brigade was to strike North along the Eastern bank of the Santerno, providing protection to the right flank of the Irish Brigade and directing itself on the bridges over the Reno South of Bastia.

As a result of developments which were taking place in the advance of the 8th Indian Division this plan was altered. The armour of 21 Tank Brigade, under command of the Indian Division, was to penetrate deeply into the enemy's territory between the Senio and the Santerno during the night of April 10th and it was anticipated that the right flank operation which was to have been the role of 36 Brigade would be largely unnecessary. Accordingly, the Divisional Commander decided to pass 36 Brigade foremost into the Santerno bridgehead and to employ it as an offensive force to operate on the left flank of the Irish Brigade. It was certain by this time that the effort of the Corps would be directed northward, in a punch aimed directly at Argenta, the hinge of the enemy's line of defence.

As a necessary preliminary to these future operations the Division was to be concentrated between the Santerno and the Senio in an area where a successful "marriage" of infantry and armour could take place. Great care had been taken in the planning stage that there should be no hitches in this "marriage". Provisional areas near Lugo, which had been nicknamed "Wedding-areas", had been allotted to each of the two forward brigades. Here infantry and armour were to form up in their battle order, with assault engineer troops and every supporting element. Thither they were to come from their non-operational concentrations east of the Senio, and thence they were to depart, in battle array, to cross into the Santerno bridgehead and break out into the enemy's deeper defences.

By evening on April 10th the leading divisions had made strides between the two rivers and had passed the town of Lugo. Orders were received at Divisional headquarters to move across the Senio early on April 11th and be ready for a move forward from the "Wedding-areas" on the same afternoon — a formidable movement problem. Therefore, it was planned that the bulk of the transport should be passed over the Senio bridges in the Indian Division's sector while fullest possible use was to be made of the bridge which was being constructed by the Division's own engineers near Cotignola.

At 1900 hours 10th April the CRE reported that this bridge would be capable of passing traffic from 2030 hours onwards in case of emergency, but that it would not be completed to the best advantage until midnight. It was estimated that its capacity would be limited to 150 vehicles per hour, due to the difficult approaches. The bridge was to be known as "Felix".

Later in the evening plans were changed in detail and it was decided that tanks would be passed across a bridge in the New Zealand Division's sector, whilst those wheeled vehicles which could not be sent over "Felix" bridge would make use of one being built by 5th Corps Engineers on the main road from Bagnacavallo to Lugo.

In the early hours of the morning on April 11th the plans for operations were confirmed in a message from the 5th Corps which read as follows:—

"From: MAIN 5 CORPS   10 2300 B
Action: 78 DIV — 2 NZ DIV — 8 IND DIV — 51 BLU
Infm: 56 DIV — 1 AGRA — 2 AGRA — A ARMD REGT RE — 5 C TPS RE — 5 C SIGS — MAIN EIGHTH ARMY — 10 CORPS — ADC — GS1 — G(AIR) — G(SD) — DA & QMG — A — Q — RA — RE — CSO — MOV — MAIU(WEST) — PHANTOM — WD 2.

0.960 SECRET (.) OPERATIONS beyond R SANTERNO (.)

ONE (.)   78 DIV will be prepared to pass through 8 IND DIV p m 11 apr (.) div will have leading bde gp conc in LUGO at two hrs notice to move wef 1100 hrs 11 apr (.) codeword for passing through MILNER (.)

TWO (.)   axes beyond R SANTERNO.
        (A) 78 DIV WEST of R SANTERNO to BASTIA (.)
        (B) 2 NZ DIV MASSA LOMBARDA — T SILLARO 2145 — SCOLO SILLARO 1849 — T QUADERNA 1253 — TORRENTE IDICE at 0957 — MOLINELLA 1561 — X rds 073750 (.)

THREE (.)   bdy beyond R SANTERNO wef MILNER 303417 — all incl 78 DIV rd junc 285444 — SCOLO ZANIOLO 264470 NORTH down SCOLO to R RENO thence R RENO to 19 EASTING (.) divs will arrange mutually if 2 NZ DIV require crossings over SCOLO ZANIOLO in S PATRIZIO area (.)

FOUR (.)   bdys for conc of 78 DIV effective from 0600 hrs 11 apr (.)
        (A) bdy between 8 IND DIV and 78 DIV as at present to rly at 386378 thence all incl 78 DIV rd junc 386379 thence rd to rd junc 361385 thence R SENIO to 358396 thence excl 78 DIV X rds 323406 (.)
        (B) bdy between 78 DIV and 2 NZ DIV as at present to R SENIO thence rly to all incl 78 DIV rd at 359360 — rd junc 349367 thence as present right bdy 2 NZ DIV (.)

FIVE (.)   78 DIV will control all routes and allotment of areas within bdys as in para FOUR but will NOT displace operational units without permission divs concerned (.)

SIX (.)   tank mov (.) 2 NZ DIV will allot tank route to 78 DIV to enable tks to move from present 78 DIV area to LUGO wef 0900 hrs 11 apr (.) this route suitable tks ONLY (.) 78 DIV will liaise closely with 8 IND DIV also in case necessary to use another tk route (.)

SEVEN (.)   ARTY (.) RA 78 DIV incl 11 RHA will revert to comd 78 DIV at 0800 hrs 11 apr (.) on completion of moves to area as required by 78 DIV this arty will continue to sp 2 NZ DIV until 78 DIV is operationally committed (.) orders re med regts follow (.)

EIGHT (.)   5 NORTHAMPTONS will revert to comd 78 DIV at 1800 hrs 11 apr from which time 5 NORTHAMPTONS will be prepared to move to 78 DIV area on orders that div (.)

NINE (.)   CREMONA ICG will take over responsibility of 5 NORTHAMPTONS front by 1800 hrs 11 apr (.) ACK all infm.

If liable to interception by enemy this   Priority   THI..........
   message must be sent IN CIPHER   SDR to
       (Signed) ARW LOW, BGS.   action addressees

By dawn on April 11th everything was ready. "Felix" bridge, which had been constructed by 237 Field Company RE, was open for traffic up to class 40 and exceeded all expectations in its ability to clear traffic quickly. As a result, the guns of 138 Field Regiment were able to be fed into the stream of traffic and crossed the river well ahead of schedule.

A traffic control organisation, in touch by wireless with Divisional Headquarters, regulated the movement at crucial points and paid a high dividend on the outlay of energy and resources.

The provost, as usual, were the salt of the earth and quietly worked their customary miracles wherever there was a block or a muddle.

The Division moved forward.

With the leading divisions the fighting had progressed swiftly during the past 12 hours. By 0700 hours on the 11th forward troops of the New Zealand Division were barely short of the Santerno and it was expected that they would cross it during the next few hours. On the right the Indians were also approaching the river and it seemed probable that during the day the whole Corps front would roll forward and close upon the Santerno line.

By nightfall this had, in fact, happened; and more also. The Indians, having assaulted the river with the 17th Indian Infantry Brigade leading, had succeeded in establishing a foothold on the western bank by 1400 hours just to the south of San Lorenzo. Earlier in the day the New Zealanders, as had been anticipated, had forced a crossing south of the Lugo-Massa Lombarda railway and had expanded this bridgehead steadily during the day.

The 78th Division was, by this time, concentrated around the town of Lugo, less 11 Brigade Group and Buffs which were still east of the Senio.

This was an important time: it was vital that everything should be in readiness to press on. The leading troops of the Corps had already broken the enemy's hold on what might have been his most formidable line of natural defence — the Santerno river —, and the success of the whole offensive depended upon one factor — momentum.

The intention of the 15th Army Group in launching the offensive was to "destroy the enemy south of the Po". So far he had been driven back and had suffered a hard knock but his positions on the Santerno were a fine cushion on which to fall back. Hinged, as the were, on the river Reno in the north and following the line of the Santerno southwards into the mountains these natural positions were all that the enemy desired as a backbone for his defences.

Here, however, he reaped the harvest of his tenacious stand on the untenable banks of the Senio. The Santerno, like the Senio, had been subjected to "carpet" bombing to an extent rightly called "saturation", and all this just at the time when it was necessary to muster every man to hold the line. Struck at from the air and harried between the two rivers by the relentless and brilliant progress of the New Zealanders and the Indians, he had failed to keep the front intact: there was a crack; the Indians and the New Zealanders were forcing it slowly open; the momentum of attack must be kept up at all costs.

In order that he might be able, at just such a moment as this, to unleash new pressure, the Corps Commander had held in his reserve until this time a formidable striking force. The moment was nearing when this force, this new sharp weapon, was to be pushed through and thrust about into the enemy's vitals: it is suitable at this juncture to examine its composition.

CHAPTER III.

Composition of the 78th Division.

On the evening of April 11th the 78th Division had under its command the following additional troops :—

2 Armoured Brigade less 10 H
11 RHA
4 H less 'C' Squadron
48 Royal Tanks
'B' Squadron 51 Royal Tanks ("Flails")
'C' Squadron 51 Royal Tanks ("Crocodiles")
24 Army Field Regiment RA (Self-propelled guns)
Half 'E' Assault Squadron RE
Detachment of 'H' Assault Squadron RE.

The outline grouping of the Division's fighting forces was as follows :—

11 British Infantry Brigade (Commander — Brigadier G. E. Thubron, DSO, OBE.)

Under command
- 2 LF
- 1 Surreys
- 5 Northamptons
- 255 Anti-tank Battery (64 Anti-tank Regiment)
- 'B' Support Group (1 Kensingtons).

In support
- 132 Field Regiment RA on and after 15 April
- 237 (Highland) Field Company RE.

36 Infantry Brigade (Comander — Brigadier G. R. D. Musson. DSO.)

Under command
- 5 Buffs
- 6 RWK
- 8 A & SH
- 48 Royal Tanks
- 'C' Squadron 56 Recce Regiment
- 256 Anti-tank Battery (64 Anti-tank Regiment)
- One troop (SP guns) 209 Anti-tank Battery (64 Anti-tank Regiment)
- 'C' Support Group (1 Kensingtons)

In support
- 138 Field Regiment RA
- 256 Field Company RE

38 (Irish) Infantry Brigade (Commander — Brigadier T. P. D. Scott, DSO.)

Under command
- 2 Innisks
- 2 LIR
- 1 R IR F
- 2 Armoured Brigade (Commander — Brigadier J. F. B. Combe, DSO.)
  - 9 L
  - 11 RHA
  - Bays
- 4 H ("Kangaroos") less 'C' Squadron
- 'A' Squadron 56 Recce Regiment
- 'B' Squadron 51 Royal Tanks ("Flails")
- 'C' Squadron 51 Royal Tanks ("Crocodiles")
- 254 Anti-tank Battery (64 Anti-tank Regiment)
- One SP Troop 209 Anti-tank Battery (64 Anti-tank Regiment)
- Half 'E' Assault Squadron RE
- Detachment of 'H' Assault Squadron RE
- 'D' Support Group (1 Kensingtons)

In support
- 214 Field Company RE
- 17 Field Regiment RA

Under direct command 78th Division:

56 Recce Regiment (Commander — Lt. Col. R. M. W. Hartland-Mahon, MC.) (less 'A' and 'C' Squadrons).

1 Kensingtons (Commander — Lt. Col. B. L. Bryar.) (less 'B', 'C' and 'D' Support Groups).

In support 78th Division:

2 AGRA (of which 73rd Medium Regiment RA — (one battery 4.5," one battery 5.5") was in direct support divisional artillery and under comand for movement.

214/57 HAA Regt RA (under command for movement)
155/52 LAA Regt RA (under command for movement)
Y Survey Tp, 5 Survey Regt RA
'A' Flight, 654 Air OP Squadron.

8th Indian Divisional Artillery (in direct support for break-out and again 15th—20th April).

CHAPTER IV.

The break-out from he Santerno bridgehead.

During the night 11/12 April the "form" on the Corps front was beginning to crystallise. The 8th Indian Division had elements of five battalions of the 17th and 21st Indian Infantry Brigades over the Santerno and the bridgehead could be said to be firm although small. No bridges were yet in operation due to trouble which had been encountered in bringing equipment up to the water's edge. The proposed bridging area was still under fire from enemy machine-guns and mortars, but the Indians were confident that during the early morning hours they would be able to establish a foothold in depth and bridge the river with an "Ark". This confidence proved itself to be well founded: the "Ark" was in position by 0530 hours and less than an hour later a troop of tanks, having crossed the bridge, had penetrated a thousand yards beyond the river without meeting any really serious resistance. The infantry were engaged in wide and solid expansion of their gains, and the enemy's movements indicated that he was trying to carry out a general withdrawal.

On the left, the New Zealanders' bridgehead was also firm, although, as light first dawned, there were still many enemy in positions close around it. In bridging they had been more fortunate than their neighbours. They had one class 40 bridge working before darkness began to lift and by first light tanks were already across together with anti-tank guns and carriers.

During the morning a steady extension of the gains developed, while the enemy withdrew his armour and infantry as best he could from what had been a decisive failure. At mid-day the two bridgeheads linked up and the 8th Indian Division's area beyond the river grew rapidly thereafter.

Just before two o'clock in the afternoon the order was received from Corps headquarters that the 78th Division would pass into the bridgehead of the 8th Indian Division at once. The Divisional Commander ordered the 36th Infantry Brigade Group to begin its move forward.

The plan was as follows. 36 Brigade, with 48 R.Tks from 21 Tank Brigade (under command 8th Indian Division) and one squadron of 56 Recce Regiment, was to cross the river and extend the Indians' bridgehead to the west. This done, 38 (Irish) Brigade Group, with the main weight of the Divisions' armour under its command, was to pass over and form up facing northwards. The remainder of 56 Recce Regiment was to operate in conformity with any advance of the Irish Brigade, but on the east side of the river, in the role which had initially been envisaged for 36 Brigade.

From the time that the word "go" was given at 1400 hours events moved rapidly forward. The Commander of 36 Brigade made his plan and ordered 8 A & SH to cross the river forthwith, supported by 'B' squadron of 48 R.Tks. This force, together with 'C' squadron 56 Recce Regiment, was to capture the group of houses known as Tre Case, 1000 yards beyond the most forward troops of the Indian Division. Having reached this objective it was to push on to the Scolo Fossatone and thence, if possible, exploit northwards towards the village of Conselice.

With great speed, considering the congestion of the traffic, the battalion group succeeded in reaching its forming-up area on the west bank of the river by mid-afternoon. The squadron of tanks had difficulty on the road, and arrangements for artillery support of the attack were also a cause of anxiety at one time, due to the speed with which everything had had to be done. Despite all, the attack was launched at 1730 hours, and the infantry with two companies up moved steadily forward behind a barrage, supported by their tanks. Little opposition was met and at 1855 hours Tre Case was reached and passed. By 1940 hours the leading infantry were on the line of the Scolo Fossatone and every indication pointed to a general withdrawal of the enemy.

As soon as 8 A & SH with their supporting troops, had crossed the river, 38 Brigade, with the armoured "Kangaroo" carriers and tanks, began to follow on. 1 R IR F, with the Queen's Bays, crossed soon after six o'clock in the evening and formed up in the northern part of the bridgehead. 2 Innisks, the next to cross, were delayed by shelling on the bridge and a general congestion of traffic. They arrived finally just as it was getting dark and the Divisional Commander decided that it was too late to launch the general attack northwards that night. The battalions went into harbour areas around Mondaniga and fighting patrols were planned for the night to probe the enemy defences in preparation for an armoured advance in the morning.

36 Brigade's operation, meanwhile, was developing successfully against light and scattered opposition. The Argylls were still fresh and it was decided that the advantage would be pressed on through the night independent of the Irish Brigade. This was "offensive flank protection" indeed!

The Brigade Commander ordered the battalion to strike out northwestwards from its positions on the line of the Fossatone dyke, and sieze the village of San Patrizio, on the road to Conselice. Little opposition had been met so far in the advance but the operation was hazardous nevertheless as the left flank was widely exposed. The New Zealanders had made great steps forward from their bridgehead and were, in fact, attacking the town of Massa Lombarda at this time, but they had not extended their front far to the north and a gap of nearly five thousand yards lay on the left flank of the Brigade's proposed line of advance.

A salient factor in the appreciation, however, was the enemy's state of disorganisation. The rapid advance from the Senio to the Santerno had thrown him from his poise, and the shattering "carpet" bombing of the whole Santerno line had served to destroy his balance altogether. He had had no time to regain his grip before the ground forces were assaulting across the river and making firm their bridgeheads. At this point he might well have expected that we should pause to draw up our tails, consolidate the bridgeheads deliberately, and launch a further punch with carefully prepared plans. Had this been done it seems most likely that success would have been more costly; the precious momentum would have been lost and equally precious time would have been given to the enemy to organise his resources, and to mount a counter-attack.

As it was, this was the moment when the fresh weapon was unsheathed, and by the rapid expansion of the Indian Division's bridgehead it was possible to penetrate deeply into his zone of defence and yet meet only scattered and harassed elements of his forces.

By 2020 hours the Argylls had crossed the Scolo Fossatone, working in close co-operation with their squadron of Churchill tanks, and reached new objectives at Zeppa Nuova and Zeppa Superiore nearly one thousand yards west of the dyke.

There was fighting before these two objectives were taken, and before the end both were burning fiercely in the night.

The advance was pressed on and after some further sharp encounters with enemy infantry and some tanks, San Patrizio was reached by 2130 hours. During this advance the Argylls made the most of the armour fighting with them, both as vehicles and as guns. Travelling on the tanks they fired their automatic weapons on the enemy positions, all the while moving forward and finally over-running what little organised resistance was met.

The benefit of the rapid three-mile thrust was evident at once. The enemy was patently in a state of disruption. Trees all along the route, which had been prepared for felling and would have slowed our rate of advance had they been turned into obstacles, were left standing. Shortly after arriving in San Patrizio a "Rhinoceros" self-propelled gun rumbled into the village; the German crew climbed out and came over to speak to men of one of the Churchill tanks which, in the half-darkness, they took to be one of their own. Their surprise on being taken prisoner was typical of the general state of the enemy's defence.

Up to this time the operation had yielded a bag of 20 prisoners, some three enemy tanks knocked out, and the "Rhinoceros" captured intact. Three miles of valuable ground had been gained and, in all, there was good cause for satisfaction.

The success of this small operation was not to be allowed to prove barren. The Divisional Commander ordered 36 Brigade to press on and take the important village of Conselice at the earliest possible time. 6 RWK, who had originally been warned for a move forward from their concentration area near Lugo at 0400 hours, were alerted at midnight and ordered to move at once. They started at 0200 hours (April 13th), with 'C' Squadron of 48 R.Tks, and passed over the river and on to San Patrizio where they arrived in their vehicles shortly before dawn.

By this time the Argylls had made firm the whole area of the village, and had secured the two bridges over the Canale dei Molini further west. Little difficulty had been encountered in securing these points, although there was activity at the southern bridge in the early hours of the morning when a party of six enemy approached, presumably with the intention of demolition. The party was accounted for before it could do any damage, and likewise two enemy armoured cars which drove up shortly afterwards, but reversed in haste. Further attempts were discouraged by the brens of the Argylls which continued to sweep the area of the road until daylight.

Despite the lack of coherent enemy activity in this area, it was thought that Conselice would be a tougher nut to crack. Just to the west of the town lay the last bridge over the Molini canal before this waterway joined the Reno river five miles further north. For all the enemy troops south of the Reno and still east of the canal this was the last way out to the west. How many enemy there were in this pocket it was hard to estimate, but it was certain that he would keep his way out open until the last possible moment.

This thought in mind, 6 RWK set out from San Patrizio in the lifting darkness at 0520 hours: the battalion was supported by a squadron of 48 R.Tks. An hour later two companies were 500 yards short of Conselice and encountering bitter opposition. One troop of the tanks succeeded in knocking out two enemy self-propelled guns, but itself sustained a casualty, the troop-leader being killed and his tank receiving a direct hit on the turret. The encounter was at close range; immediately the enemy saw his success a small party dashed forward and boarded the tank. A moment later it was driven away complete with the remainder of its crew, if these survived, and carrying code documents and equipment. It was found later, abandoned north of the village.

As always in his rearguard actions, the enemy made great and effective use of his self-propelled guns. Throughout the morning of the 13th scattered pockets of infantry, fighting with the support of these guns, engaged our own forces in a fierce struggle for the approaches to the town. Some 20 or more prisoners were taken but no decision was reached in the fighting and it was impossible to push on. At 0945 hours the Air Force had been called upon and engaged, with gratifying effect, some guns in the eastern outskirts of the town. The nut, however, remained uncracked.

Turning now to the Irish Brigade's sector, the main axis of advance for the Division, the fight had begun in earnest. In the early hours of the 13th the brigade launched its long-planned attack with two battalions up; on the right 2 Innisks, on the left 1 R.Ir.F. Each battalion was supported by a squadron of the Queen's Bays (Sherman Tanks), and a troop of "Crocodiles" (Flame-throwing Churchills) from 'C' Squadron 51 R.Tks. In addition, engineer assault equipment was available to assist the movement of the armour.

The start line running west from San Lorenzo was bounded on the right by the river Santerno with its high flood bank, and on the left by the Fossatone canal. The plan was as follows. The two infantry battalions, each with its armoured squadron, were to force a passage northwards between the two waterways as far as the Scolo di Conselice which crossed the line of advance some 7,500 yards to the north. Having reached this point, which was, in fact, almost at the apex of a narrow triangle whose base was the start-line, the bridge giving access northwards was to be siezed and the "Kangaroo Force" passed through. It was a straight-forward plan, bold and simple and in perfect unison with the higher plan to strike swiftly at the pivot of the enemy's defence, Argenta.

The initial frontage of the attack was little over 2,000 yards and both battalions were engaged in stubborn fighting, pushing the enemy back in a slow drive lasting two and a half hours. By mid-morning approximately half the distance to the Conselice Canal had been covered, and the frontage between the two waterways had shrunk to 1000 yards. Numerous enemy strong-points were encountered, and these appeared to be getting harder to overcome as the front narrowed.

With the Inniskillings just short of San Bernardino, and engaged in liquidating a very troublesome enemy post on the river-side, the Irish Fusiliers were directed westwards, and crossed the Fossatone canal shortly before 1100 hours. The advance was then continued on a broader front as the Inniskillings approached closer to San Bernardino, and the Fusiliers came up level with them on the left.

The village itself proved troublesome. The 8th Indian Division attacked it on the east of the Santerno and the Inniskillings fought for the western portion but the enemy's 362nd Infantry Division, although tired, disorganised, and short of everything it required, was putting up a stout defence. The village was finally overrun, both to the east and west of the river, and it was reported clear at 1300 hours.

By this time the leading troops of the two Irish battalions had made further progress on the left and had reached the village of La Giovecca. This was occupied by 2 Innisks and the road thence to the east was cleared for a short distance. 1 R.Ir.F. were level with their sister-battalion on the left of the Fossatone canal and were facing west to protect a flank which had by now become exposed as 36 Brigade fought for Conselice. On the right, East of the Santerno 'A' Squadron of the Recce Regiment pressed northwards in conformity with the Irish Brigade, under whose command it had been placed at 0730 hours that morning.

While these events were taking place many moves had been made further back in preparation for the future. 5 Buffs and 56 Recce Regiment less 'A' Squadron had been moved up to join 36 Brigade in the area of San Patrizio, the Regiment passing to under command of this Brigade on its arrival at approximately 1120 hours. At the same time 11 Brigade was being moved up from the back areas, where it had been held since the first assault, and was concentrating in the area of Lugo.

To return to the Irish Brigade, however; at 1300 hours the Inniskillings and Royal Irish Fusiliers, although they had not reached the apex of their triangle, were ordered to consolidate positions in preparation for the "Kangaroo" Force to pass through.

Soon afterwards this move began. Under command of 2 Armoured Brigade the force of armour and infantry, composed of the 9th Lancers and the 2nd

London Irish Rifles in the "Kangaroo" carriers of 'A' Squadron of the 4th Hussars, debouched from the positions held by the Inniskillings and advanced towards the bridge at Cavamento, the apex of the original triangle. The ponderous mass of vehicles took some time to manoeuvre through La Giovecca and the afternoon was drawing on before the force was in full cry.

Resistance at first was patchy and undecided. Here and there parties of enemy with "Bazookas" caused trouble, and one tank was lost by fire from an anti-tank gun early in the battle. On the whole, however, it appeared that the enemy was shaken; his grip everywhere was loosening.

By mid-afternoon the leading elements of the force were approaching the canal. The right flank was no longer limited by the Santerno river, and this gave more room for manoeuvre. H Company came up on the left of 'G' Company, together with 'C' Squadron 9 L.

Determined resistance was met in the village of La Frascata, just before the canal, but 'G' Company dealt with this and 'H' Company was able to drive straight through in its Kangaroos. Reaching the canal bank the leading tanks were just in time to see the bridge blown up immediately in front of them. The infantry dismounted at once from their Kangaroos and, under cover of fire from their supporting tanks, crossed the canal on the remains of the road and railway bridges and rushed the houses on the north side. More prisoners were taken, and a surprised and shaken enemy was hunted down in areas which had been by-passed by the swift thrust.

'H' Company was ordered to hold the bridgehead over the canal with assistance from 'E' Company which was also engaged in clearing La Frascata. 'G' Company was clearing the area up to the canal bank on the right.

At 1830 hours 2 Armoured Brigade reported two troops of 9 L across the canal where the bridge, although badly damaged, had not been utterly destroyed and was just passable for tracks. Mopping up and consolidation were in progress, and the Engineers were at work making a new road bridge under cover of the infantry and tanks.

On the left 36 Brigade was still engaged in stiff fighting. Little material progress had been made in Conselice during the day, where the enemy was firmly ensconced. As a result of the rapid advance of the Irish Brigade on the right a gap had appeared in the Division's front between the two brigades. 6 RWK were fully deployed in the area of Conselice, and one company of the 5th Buffs was, therefore, brought up to fill the gap. This was complete by 1630 hours.

At about this time the enemy mounted a strong counter-attack upon 6 RWK from out of Conselice, and fierce fighting raged for an hour or more. The headquarter buildings of two forward platoons were hit by enemy shells and set on fire, but the attack was eventually beaten off just before sundown.

The general indications on this left flank seemed to show the enemy as determined to hold his ground: a firmness of intention in his defence was apparent for the first time. It was therefore decided that a co-ordinated attack by the whole Brigade would be necessary, and the remainder of 5 Buffs was ordered to move to San Patrizio at once.

As last light fell there was a temporary halt on the whole of the Divisional front; the day's gains were being consolidated on the right, whilst 36 Brigade prepared to clear up Conselice and the surrounding area on the left by a deliberate attack.

The plan of the 36th Brigade's Commander was to push northwestwards to cut the road from Conselice to Chiesanova, and subsequently to clear the town of Conselice itself. To this end the Argylls were to attack in a preliminary operation and clear the area to the southwest of Conselice; 5 Buffs were then to pass through and cut the Conselice — Chiesanova road; finally, at first light, 6 RWK were to clear the town.

By 2245 hours the Argylls reached their objectives with little difficulty, taking seven prisoners and losing only one man wounded. The Buffs passed through at once and met no opposition to their thrust across the road. At the same time information was received from civilians that the enemy had departed from the town, although he had probably not gone far back. 5 Buffs were ordered to push on to Chiesanova, and 6 RWK to confirm that Conselice was clear. By 0330 hours the Buffs had reached Chiesanova and the RWK were moving into Conselice without opposition. Civilians confirmed that the enemy had withdrawn during the early hours of the morning. Half an hour later the leading company of the Buffs was 1000 yards beyond Chiesanova moving northwestwards and it looked as if the whole of the western portion of the Division's sector would shortly be clear as far as the river Sillaro, with the exception of pockets and isolated posts still to be mopped up.

Accordingly, at first light next morning the Commander of 36 Brigade ordered 56 Recce Regiment, which had been placed under his command on the previous day, to pass through the positions of 8 A & SH and 5 Buffs and exploit westwards up to the Sillaro on the whole Brigade front.

Taking stock on the morning of April 14th there was good ground for solid satisfaction. To the right, north of the Reno, the 56th (London) Division was coming into view moving due westwards towards Bastia and Argenta. Between this thrust and the northward drive of the Irish and 2nd Armoured Brigades, the Italian "Cremona" Combat Group had crossed the Santerno without opposition and was moving forward on Route 16, also towards Bastia. The 8th Indian Division, across whose front the Irish Brigade had moved, was now out of the fighting and being concentrated in the Corps reserve.

On the left the New Zealanders were still pressing vigorously forward and had established a small bridgehead over the Sillaro. Between them and 36 Brigade was a wide expanse of marshy land where minor operations by 56 Recce Regiment and other troops of both divisions continued until the whole area was clear.

The 13th had indeed an unlucky day — for the enemy.

Before first light on the 14th patrols of 2 LIR under 2 Armoured Brigade's command were feeling their way forward towards Lavezzola and the Reno. At dawn they were followed by the armour in two columns, one working due north on the axis of the main road, the other sweeping round to the right of Lavezzola, which was known to be heavily mined. Both columns were directed on the approaches to the Bastia bridges. The column moving through Lavezzola found mines in profusion, and houses in the northern part of the village booby-trapped. Fortunately the enemy's departure had been so hasty that he had been unable to remove the warning notices from the danger areas and not a single casualty was caused either to armour or to infantry. The "Flail" tanks of 51 R.Tks. had a great morning exploding everything they could find. In addition to mines and booby-traps the sweep yielded about 30 prisoners, 8 of whom were taken in the act of further minelaying.

At 0940 hours the Reno was reached. Both the road and railway bridges were found demolished, but sufficient rubble remained at the site of the latter to enable the infantry to get across dryshod. Recconnaissance was carried out and a plan evolved for two platoons of 2 LIR to cross the river and form a small bridgehead. This was later to be increased in strength to the extent of two companies.

At 1230 hours the operation began and the two platoons crossed under cover of smoke without difficulty. Advancing north from the far bank, however, the leading platoon was counter-attacked strongly by the enemy and most of it was over-run. No assistance could be given to this party by the tanks on the south bank of the river owing to the height of the floodbanks and, until a bridge was built, it was impossible to move the armour across. The two platoons were, therefore, withdrawn across the river, positions were taken up on the 'near' bank, patrols were sent out east and west, and recconnaissance was carried out with a view to making a deliberate assault.

In addition to reaching the Reno, 9 L had patrolled early in the morning towards Route 16 where it approached the Bastia area from the southeast. Here they had made contact with the Cremona Group at 0930 hours, thus filling in a piece of the wider picture.

A similar move was made by 48 R Tks with 36 Brigade, a patrol of Honey tanks being sent north from Conselice along the road leading to Lavezzola. This they found heavily mined but it was cleared during the day with Engineer assistance and contact was made with the Irish Brigade in Lavezzola at 1730 hours.

Further to the left 56 Recce Regiment fanned out during the day to close with the enemy all along the front on the line of the Sillaro. Contact was made in the area of the river where the enemy infantry was established in well dug-in positions and a great number of mines were encountered. 'B' and 'C' Squadrons were ordered to establish defensive positions to cover this river flank during the afternoon, and shortly afterwards 'A' Squadron reverted to command from 38 Brigade and moved to rejoin the Regiment.

By nightfall "tidying up", "mopping up" and consolidation were the orders of the day. The Santerno was far behind and had ceased to have a "bridgehead". All along the front there was a general loosening of the enemy's resistance as he readjusted his positions and fell back on his main line of defence based on Argenta. Again, therefore, there was that urgent need for maintenance of the impetus; somehow the whole weight of the Corps had to be brought to bear without delay on the defences before Argenta, and to do this there must be a bridge, and the Reno must be crossed.

It was now exactly five days since the offensive began. The operations had progressed with a steady tenor of success and very largely on lines which had been foreseen: in short, everything was going "according to plan". The sum of the achievement was that the enemy had been forced back from his winter line on the Senio with such weight and drive in the attack that he had never been in a position to reform and hold a second line. The whole area had been cleared from the Senio to the Santerno, and from the Santerno to the Reno and Sillaro; Argenta was but a mile or two ahead and already one foot of the attack was well established north of the Reno where the 56th Division was on the point of linking up with the leading elements of the Irish Brigade at Bastia. Away on the left the Fifth Army's offensive was just beginning and Bologna was almost in sight.

Another phase was ended and it was hard to foresee the form which subsequent operations would take.

CHAPTER V.

The breaking of the Argenta Gap.

The focal point of interest was now the narrow strip of land known as the Argenta Gap. Its tactical importance can be seen from a glance at the map. Briefly it was as follows.

The enemy's defences south of the Po ran from the coast into the mountains south of Bologna. Initially they had been secured on his left by the Commacchio Lake, but the operations of the 56th Division and the 2nd Commando Brigade had forced him to fall back in this sector and his line was thus cut adrift at one end. The advance from the Senio and across the Santerno had caused the wholesale withdrawal of his front and, in order to stave off a major and strategic disaster, it was essential for him to find a firm pivot on which his whole line in the eastern sector of the plain could turn. This was the more urgent at this time as the forces of the Polish Corps south of Bologna, and of the Fifth Army further to the west, were loosening his hold on the mountains. Even if the whole front around Bologna should start to crumble, as indeed he felt it might, he still required that firmness between the mountains and the Adriatic so that an escape route might be kept open.

The main thrust of the Eighth Army from the opening of the offensive onwards was directed on Ferrara and the crossings of the Po to the north of this town. Once these were lost there was great likelihood that all the enemy forces in the plain south of the river would be lost. Where, then, was he to halt our thrust on Ferrara?

The threat was developing from the south-east. Route 16, or subsidiary roads in alignment with it, was the likely axis and on this line an ideal piece of country had been selected for defensive works. To the east was flooded land stretching away to the northern part of the Commacchio Lake, with no main roads and few minor ones that were passable for heavy traffic. To the south-west a further tract of flooded waste stretched almost to Bologna. The natural obstacles in both areas had been increased by artifical flooding and demolitions. All this had been done by the enemy months before, causing no inconvenience to his lines of communication, and requiring comparatively little labour.

The stretch of land which remained was between two and three miles wide, and four miles in depth: a narrow funnel between the marshes. Careful thought was put into the organisation of defences for this strip of land, the Argenta Gap. Mines were laid thickly and in depth; houses were fortified; every bridge was prepared for demolition; an extensive network of trenches and wire linked together the native dykes, canals, and ditches, to make a corrugated passageway incapable of being rushed by tanks or infantry.

Given the men to occupy the defences and the time to get them there the enemy was confident that the block would hold and, in the worst possible case, a temporary halt would be achieved before we could turn his flanks with a ponderous semi-amphibious plunge on either side.

His appreciation was a fair one; the position was strong: there was only one "but"; could he organise his forces in time? On the evening of April 14th the matter was about to be put to the test.

It had become evident to the Corps Commander earlier in the day that to wait for a bridge to be built over the Reno before the 78th Division could add its weight to that of the 56th in assaulting the gap, would create a danger of losing the speed and momentum which was so vital. Accordingly, orders had been issued for one brigade of the 78th Division to move at once through Alfonsine to the north side of the Reno and take over the left sector of the 56th Division's front.

Late in the evening 11 Brigade moved north. That night it concentrated north-west of Alfonsine with one battalion over the Reno.

In order further to liberate the Division in the sector between Bastia and the New Zealand Division's right flank, the 2nd Commando Brigade was placed under command and began to take over the commitments of 36 Brigade which was still on the left flank.

In the Irish Brigade's sector there was little activity save for patrolling and an historic event when the 1st and 2nd Battalions of the London Irish Rifles met, side by side, for the first time on a common battle-ground. This was occasioned by the approach of 167 Brigade on the north bank of the Reno, with the 1st Battalion leading on the left.

The 15th and 16th were days of vast activity in regrouping and movement. 11 Brigade was moving through 167 Brigade in the area north of the Reno, remote from the rest of the Division by reason of the lack of a bridge. 167 Brigade, less two battalions, came under temporary command of 78 Division on the 15th and reverted to command of the 56th Division the next morning. The 2nd Commando Brigade completed the relief of 36 Brigade, but remained under command of 78th Division. The Recce Regiment passed to under direct command of 5 Corps, and returned again to the Division's command shortly afterwards.

By the evening of April 16th solid achievements emerged. 11 Brigade with the Queen's Bays, and "Crocodiles" and "Flails" from 51 R Tanks under command, had passed through 167 Brigade, with 1 Surreys leading on the right and 5 Northamptons on the left. 2 LF followed in brigade reserve. The advance had been made astride the railway and positions had been reached just short of the

Fosso Marina, a canal which ran across the full width of the gap and was considered as a likely main line of the enemy's resistance.

Meanwhile, the Engineers of 214 Field Company had succeeded in the not inconsiderable task of bridging the Reno; 38 Brigade had crossed to concentrate southeast of the gap; 2 Armoured Brigade had also crossed, and Divisional Headquarters followed.

11 Brigade's advance had been rapid and only lightly opposed, but extensive minefields had been encountered throughout, gradually thickening as the Fosso Marina was approached. On reaching the outskirts of Argenta, and the line of this canal enemy resistance became firm and a full scale assault was clearly going to be required.

The plan evolved was that after dark 1 Surreys would move forward on the right and secure a firm base from which 2 LF would assault the canal and press through to outflank the town.

The preliminary advance was successful and the Fusiliers began their assault on the strongly held enemy line. Fierce resistance was encountered at once and a long and bitter struggle ensued before any concrete gain was made. By midnight however, the Battalion had succeeded in gaining a hold on the far bank of the canal, with forward positions up to 200 yards beyond it.

No sooner was this bridgehead established than the enemy began to pound it with all that he had. Heavy shell and mortar fire came down on the area of the crossing and along the banks of the canal. Several counter-attacks were thrown in but all to no avail. The Lancashire Fusiliers stood their ground and the bridgehead, still only a tiny one, remained firm. This achievement was the first decisive step in the breaking of the gap.

Throughout the fighting the Divisional Artillery and the heavy mortars of the Kensingtons had been laying down a heavy programme of support. By some chance a relief was in progress on the enemy's side just as the fire-plan opened and large numbers of Germans were caught in the open. Only later, as the bridgehead began to expand, did the remarkable results of the fire become apparent. Both from the barrage and from defensive fire the enemy's casualities were exceptionally heavy, and this at a time when he could ill afford to lose a single man unnecessarily.

As the night wore on the sappers worked continuously on the crossing of the canal and just before dawn an "Ark" bridge was established. One troop of the Bays' tanks managed to cross but the strain proved too much for the "Ark" and it collapsed before more armour could cross. Later in the morning, however, the crossing was repaired and a satisfactory route established.

From the outset this attack had been a plain infantry slogging-match. Its success was one of those achievements that can only be accomplished by the infantry; a bitter, painful, struggle; and a solid, valuable prize though small when measured in yards.

At first light on the morning of the 17th 1 Surreys were ordered to move one company forward to protect the left flank of the Lancashire Fusiliers bridgehead. After some determined resistance had been overcome this company succeeded in establishing itself in the north-east outskirts of Argenta.

5 Northamptons, meanwhile, were holding a line on the edge of the town and acting as a pivot for the main weight of the division's attack on the right.

The enemy's position was beginning to look poor. He had failed to hold us on ground of his own choosing and he had every reason to believe that the main weight of the thrust was still to come. His forces consisted of elements of the battered 42nd Jaeger and 362nd Infantry Divisions, bolstered up at the last moment by the 29th Panzer Grenadier Division which had been rushed down from the north. The arrival of this formation was greeted by our own intelligence staff as a good omen. Evidently the enemy was feeling the draught in a big way. Not only at Argenta, nor merely in the eastern sector of the front, were things beginning to crumble away, but in the whole Italian theatre, the entire floor of the German military machine, cracks were beginning to appear which could not be plugged up. The 29th Panzer Grenadier Division was the last major field formation remaining in the Army-Group reserve.

At Argenta then, as had been expected, the enemy was going to make a desperate stand. The crust of his defence had been cracked by the Lancashire Fusiliers, and now, on the morning of April 17th no time was to be lost in pressing the advantage which that crack had given us.

The subsequent operations were of the highest consequence.

First the Irish Brigade was passed through. With 1 R Ir F leading and 2 Inniskks folowing, they passed into the bridgehead of 11 Brigade shortly before dawn and pressed determinedly on throughout the day gaining, by nightfall, about 1,000 yds to the north and the west respectively. In the area of the Scolo Arenare the Irish Fusiliers met exceptionally strong resistance, and this was not finally cleared until later.

Towards evening 11 Brigade began to set about clearing the town of Argenta itself. For this purpose 5 Northamptons were employed, with the assistance of "Crocodile" flamethrowers of 51 R Tanks. The operation was successfully completed by 2030 hours, at which time it was reported that the town was clear. In the early hours of the morning on the 18th, however, a strong counter-attack was put in by the enemy from the area of San Antonio, northwest of the town. This counter-attack appeared to be in company strength, with tank support. Eventually it was beaten off, and the enemy retreated northwards, a number of prisoners being taken by the Irish Brigade, elements of which had worked round the north edge of the town.

Further to the left of the Division's sector, and south of the Reno, 2 Commando Brigade, which was trying to push up the river bank past Argenta, had encountered vigorous opposition all day on the 17th from buildings near San Antonio. By evening no material progress had been made in this extremely difficult area.

The counter-attack in Argenta was not, however, the be-all and end-all of the night's activities. Quite on the contrary, the early hours of the 18th were chosen for the launching of the next punch to widen the crack.

11 Brigade had borne the main weight of the fighting north of the Reno and had done well; the infantry were tired. 38 Brigade with its two battalions had been committed, had fought on, had gained a further thousand yards and was also tired. This was no time to try levering the gap open with chisels which were already blunted with the contact; new, sharp instruments were required, and two were at hand.

By the arrival of the Commando Brigade 36 Brigade had been freed of all its committments south of the Reno and was ready to fight again as soon as it was needed. 2 Armoured Brigade's Kangaroo force, too, was ready to take the field again.

The Divisional Commander decided on a series of rapid punches, each to follow the other in quick succession from the right of the town, by-passing the enemy who was still holding on near San Antonio.

At 0215 hours 6 RWK passed through the lines of the Royal Irish Fusiliers and struck straight across country for the village of Boccaleone, lying on the main road through the gap and some three thousand yards past Argenta. No sooner were the infantry through the Irish Brigade's lines than a confusion of fighting began. It was difficult in the dark to know exactly where the rest of the Irishmen were, and even more difficult to keep direction whilst moving across the cultivated country, everywhere intersected with ditches, fences, wire, and minefields. Some enemy tanks were about, and further south the Northamptons were being counter-attacked in the town.

After one and a half hours had passed, and with the fog of war particularly dense that morning, the Argylls launched out in the wake of 6 RWK, and set their course for Consandolo, the next village beyond Boccaleone. This was the second thrust of the round.

If our own picture was somewhat obscure at that time one can only imagine what the enemy's maps must have shown. At dusk on the 17th he had been holding the whole of route 16 down to the outskirts of Argenta and around the town his line had curved northwest towards the railway. The situation had looked sticky for him, but not stuck. Now, at four o'clock in the morning, when he was concentrating on a counter-attack to regain the town and keep control of the main road, he suddenly found two spearheads in his side driving in from the east and directed on his main road in the back areas. There must have been discomfort in the caravans of the 29 Panzer Grenadier Division's Headquarters at that drab hour in the morning.

Above all this confusion the sun began to rise on the 18th morning and dawn revealed remarkable achievements. 6 RWK were entering Boccaleone from the east. 8 A & SH were well on their way to Consandolo, a mile or more beyond, and the enemy was in confusion; 40 or so prisoners had been brought in and many more were on their way.

Not all the enemy was fleeing however. In addition to isolated men in scattered houses who decided to fight it out, there was a solid pocket of enemy still firmly ensconced in San Antonio. With the river to the west of them, and their enemies on the other three sides their chances looked dim, but they still fought on.

In order to clear this blockage from route 16, which was to be the main line of communication for the whole Corps later on, 56 Recce Regt was placed under command of 36 Brigade and ordered to pass through Argenta and clear the enemy from San Antonio which was now on the brigade's left flank. Unfortunately the move proved hopeless, and the regiment was unable to make any progress astride the road by reason of demolitions and impossible going for vehicles.

By half past nine in the morning 6 RWK had done much mopping up in and around Boccaleone, having taken 38 more prisoners and a self-propelled gun complete. The Argylls however, were running into rougher water; having initially turned in towards route 16 too early, thus nearly clashing with their neighbours, they had been redirected northwards and soon met the fiercest resistance they had so far encountered in the offensive. Four of their supporting tanks were knocked out in quick succession. The enemy infantry were daring to come to close quarters and bayonets were used. The whole battalion area was subjected to heavy fire from artillery and mortars. Due to the closeness of the fighting it was impossible for our own guns to bring any weight of fire to bear on the enemy without danger to our own troops.

36 Brigade was not, however, alone in its offensive that morning. Following in the wake of the Argylls the Kangaroo force of 2 Armoured Brigade had set out at dawn. By 1000 hours this fanastic private army was out in the open engaging enemy tanks and SP guns beyond the Irish Fusiliers and on the right of the Argylls.

By 1100 hours the whole front was ablaze with activity. The Armoured Brigade, aiming at the twin canals Fosso di Porto and Scolo Bolognese, was forcing its way out into the open with the railway on the right and an unprotected flank on the left. Further west the Argylls were held up just short of Cosandolo by determined enemy in strong points, and to the left again was an open flank down route 16 until 6 RWK were met in Boccaleone, mopping up some difficult enemy pockets. Further south the RAF, at the request of 36 Brigade, was attacking San Antonio and shortly afterwards 56 Recce Regiment made a little progress up route 16 towards this troublesome block.

Soon after midday the Argylls, still stuck short of Consandolo, called for assistance from the air, and this was laid on in a big way. Most of the village was razed to the ground and beneath the piles of dust and rubbish many bodies of German soldiers and Italian civilians were buried. Still, however, Consandolo held out; the Brigade Commander ordered a halt and a planned assault. A quick barrage was laid down and carried the infantry in astride the road; at 1600 hours Consandolo was almost ours.

As evening came it was possible to sum up the day's achievements. Boccaleone and the ruined Consandolo were in our hands although there was still some clearing-up to be done. These two small villages on route 16, well up the neck of the gap, were prizes well worth having and formed the substance of the day's achievement; the capture of Consandolo had, in particular, been a fine performance. To the right the ground had been invested up as far as the Fossa Benvignante, and on the left all the area of Argenta had been cleared except for the San Antonio pocket.

The evening's work, then, fell into two parts: first, the exploitation of the advance beyond the Benvignante canal; second, the clearance of the pocket which still remained on route 16.

At about 1530 hours 2 Armoured Brigade had reported finding the railway bridge over the Benvignante canal and due north of Consandolo intact, but very heavy anti-tank fire had been met in the area from self-propelled guns of all calibres and little real progress had been made for two hours. As darkness drew near, however, a break-out was achieved past enemy guns firing over open sights, and through a maze of canals and ditches. By the light of numerous burning houses and with a sense of complete victory, the Lancers and the London Irish fanned out to cover Coltra and Palazzo, taking intact three bridges over the next canal. The enemy, having hung on in an attempt to stop the rot was now in a state of utter confusion; an officers' mess, a battery of 15 cm guns, a battery of 88 mm guns, numbers of individual pieces of all calibres and over 200 prisoners, were taken that evening by the Kangaroo Army. During this day remarkable captures of prisoners were made by the Divisional Artillery. The reconnaissance parties of 17 Field Regiment arrived in an area very well forward, some 1500 yards to the Northeast of Consandolo during the night, and at dawn had to clear the area of some 70 Germans; 132 Field Regiment going into action a little further East a couple of hours later took 5 officers and 53 other ranks prisoner; all these turned out to be from the artillery of the 42nd Jaeger Division; an unusual form of counter-battery achievement.

On the left, the time had come for final clearance of the enemy from route 16. It was imperative that this road should be cleared for the following day, so that the 6th Armoured Division could be passed right through our left flank, to strike direct at Ferrara.

The task of co-ordinating the clearance of the enemy from a pocket south of Boccaleone was given to the Irish Brigade and involved much detailed consideration. Almost everyone in the neighbourhood was involved — 5 Northamptons of 11 Brigade, 6 RWK from 36 Brigade, the Inniskillings, 56 Recce Regiment with 36 Brigade, and 2 Commando Brigade on the far side of the river — a thorough hotch-potch.

No matter how, an attack was planned and begun at midnight. The Commando Brigade went in from the south under a heavy barrage and was followed an hour and a half later by 2 Innisks. In vicious fighting which lasted until dawn the houses and floodbank were cleared, and by the arrival a little later of 6 RWK from the north the operations were eventually completed. This was a vital step achieved and a surprisingly difficult one it had proved.

At the same time in 36 Brigade's sector another plot was afoot. 5 Buffs, having followed up behind the Argylls as far as Consandolo, were launched out just after dark and began a memorable night's march to the north-west. They met only slight resistance and by dawn had pressed on a distance of 8 miles to the village of Benvignante, away and beyond the leading elements of the armoured forces This substantial advance, the longest on foot that was done by any battalion of the brigade in the entire operation, brought the division right out into the open, and decisively through the gap.

In the space of approximately 60 hours, by operations involving every battalion and armoured regiment of the division, on ground of the enemy's own choosing, and with the invaluable support of the air-forces throughout, the 29th Panzer-Grenadier Division, together with elements from four other enemy divisions, (the 26th Panzer, the 42nd Jaeger, the 98th Infantry and the 362nd Infantry), had been driven from their positions and thrown back into the plain before the Po. The 78th Division was out in the open, and the 6th Armoured Division was about to strike out to the west; the Argenta Gap was broken and the enemy lay, straggled out along the southern bank of the Po, vulnerable at a hundred points.

CHAPTER VI.

The advance to the Po di Volano.

The Po di Volano is a large river, not comparable, of course, with the Po itself, but nevertheless more than a fair-sized ditch. It runs due East from Ferarra and, in conjunction with its helpmate-canal, the Diversivo di Volano, it constitutes a major obstacle five miles or so short of the Po proper. It was to this water-jump that the Division was now turned; once over it we should be in the enemy's entrails; south of it we were but on the fringe.

During the night 18th/19th general activity continued over the whole front. On the extreme right 1 R Ir F moved forward on the east side of the railway and occupied the triangle of ground bounded by waterways around Casa Biscie. This move secured for the Division a firm right flank beyond the railway.

Further west, at 0400 hours, the London Irish patrolled forward from the Fosso Sabbiosola on the west of the railway and reached the twin canals Bolognese and di Porto just to the west of Portomaggiore. Here, a mile or so from the town, they found both bridges blown. In conjunction with the 9th Lancers' tanks, which joined the infantry at first light, positions were established on the near bank of the double canal.

Between the London Irish and the Royal Irish Fusiliers 'B' Squadron of 56 Recce Regiment with some of the Sherman tanks of the 4th Hussars was having a confused struggle to cross the two canals in the village of Portomaggiore itself. One of these canals was at the entry to, and the other at the exit from, the town. The crux of the position was an enemy strong point at Croatia, just north of and overlooking the town, which was holding out with such obstinacy that no progress was possible beyond the second canal, and the squadron was confined to the difficult, rubble-strewn area of the town's western outskirts.

In 36 Brigade's sector, all-round advances had been made overnight. 56 Recce Regiment, less 'B' Squadron, was still under command and had passed through the Argylls only a short time behind the Buffs. From Consandalo the regiment had swung to the west and at first had met little enemy resistance in a rapid advance. 'A' Squadron patrolled westwards during the early morning towards the Po Mortu di Primaro and the Fosso Molino, (two waterways which run south from San Nicolo Ferarese towards the flooded lands by Budrio). These patrols met firm enemy resistance on a line approximately 2 miles east of the canals, but it seemed certain that the enemy forces there were merely intended to cover the roads northwards on the west side of route 16, and were not, therefore, a direct menace to the Division's main line of advance which ran north from Consandalo.

On the extreme left flank, route 16 had been opened for normal traffic and interest in the marshy area west and south of the road waned into obscurity.

During the course of the day repeated attempts were made by 'B' Squadron of the Recce Regiment, assisted for a time by F Company of 2 LIR, to clear a way through Portomaggiore, but these were of no avail. In the afternoon 2 Armoured Brigade was ordered to establish a small infantry bridgehead in the area west of the town where it had originally hoped to sieze the two bridges.

The London Irish Rifles, to whom F Company was, by this time, returning, succeeded in establishing two small bridgeheads over the canals by 1530 hours, to a great accompaniment of smoke, high explosive, and flame from "Wasps".

As a result of this successful small operation it was decided that the main axis of the Division would follow through the bridgehead, and would not be led round through Portomaggiore.

This decision taken, it was essential to exploit the foothold rapidly and get some bridging-work in progress. Accordingly 11 Brigade,, which was entirely in Divisional reserve near Argenta, was ordered to pass into the bridgehead, enlarge it to cover bridging operations, and press on astride the railway to cross the next canal, the Nicolo. For the purpose of this operation the London Irish Rifles, already in the bridgehead, were placed under command of 11 Brigade, and the Bays passed, at the same time, to 11 Brigade's command.

By 2300 hours on the 19th 2 LIR, with great assistance from the Divisional Artillery, had successfully enlarged the two small bridgeheads, and merged them into one which covered the whole triangular area between the canals Belriguardo and Bolognese and a line north-east from Porto Rotta. The sappers started work at once on a crossing of the two canals to enable tanks to get over, and 11 Brigade prepared to cross with the Lancashire Fusiliers leading, followed by the Surreys. Each battalion was accompanied by a squadron of tanks from the Bays.

At 0145 hours 2 LF began to move across, and very soon afterwards, whilst the area was still under fire from enemy mortars, the sappers completed a bulldozed crossing of the twin canals and tanks began to pass over. The operation of moving into and through this small bridgehead proved more complicated than had been expected. Trouble was experienced in getting the wheeled vehicles over the crossing, and due to this and various other causes the advance astride the railway with two battalions up, (the Surreys on the right and the Lancashire Fusiliers on the left), did not get going until approximately 0900 hours. When it did begin, oposition proved to be stiff and going was slow. By nightfall positions were reached astride the railway on the general line of the road running south from Runco to the railway, thence westwards on the road to Montesanto as far as the Fossa Rivalda, and thence southwestwards to the twin canals di Porto and Bolognese. At the left extremity the line now joined up with the positions of 5 Buffs who had pushed on during the day, in the general direction of San Nicolo Ferarese, and had thus conformed with the main thrust beyond the twin canals.

While the main operation of 11 Brigade was going on, 5 Northamptons, who were in Brigade reserve, detached one company to join 2 Armoured Brigade. This company, together with the Sherman tank squadron of the 4th Hussars, set out at 1200 hours to assist 'B' Squadron of the Recce Regiment and achieve what the squadron alone had so far been unable to do in dislodging the enemy from Portomaggiore and Croatia on the extreme right flank. This proved a very sticky operation. In Croatia the enemy had two SP guns and plenty of ammunition; in the general area of the town he had enough men; by nightfall it looked as if progress had ceased and the enemy was still in occupation. As a result of this situation, 256 Field Company was prevented from getting to work on the north-west exit from Portomaggiore and it was here that it was essential that a bridge be soon established in order to open up the main road north to Voghenza.

Meanwhile, away on the left, a great change had taken place. Between the Division's left flank troops, (at that time 56 Recce Regiment), and the marshy waste to the west of route 16, the Armoured Division had begun to filter through on the evening of the 19th April. By early morning on the 20th, while 11 Brigade was beginning its advance north-west of Porto Rotta, 2 Lothians reached San Nicolo Ferarese, and the general situation on the left flank looked good and likely to get even better.

Progress on our own front during the 20th had been slow and by late afternoon the Divisional Commander decided that, in spite of the fact that the forward troops of 11 Brigade were still short of the Nicolo Canal, an attack must be made that night, so that the canal might be bridged before the enemy could fully regain his balance.

38 Brigade, now in reserve, was detailed for the operation and a conference was called at 11 Brigade Headquarters. There, on the side of his dingo, the Brigadier gave out his orders.

The plan was to cross the Nicolo Canal between the railway and the twin canals in the region forward of the Fosso Rivaldo over which 2 LF had already secured an intact crossing. It was known that all bridges across the Nicolo Canal were destroyed, but it was thought that, as they had been demolished cleanly at each end, it would be possible for infantry to cross by the rubble and demolished spans.

Zero hour for the attack was fixed for 0130 hours on April 21st.

The attack went in as planned with 1 R Ir F on the left, and 2 Inniskis on the right. On the north side of the railway 5 Northamptons gave protection to the right flank, and beyond the twin canals in the south 5 Buffs conformed with the advance. Both Irish battalions moved forward quickly behind the gunners' barrage and by 0220 hours two companies from each were across the canal, having used the rubble of the demolished bridges as stepping-stones. Oposition was far lighter than had been expected, many enemy having probably withdrawn as the barrage approached. By 0500 hours the bridgehead was 800 yards deep, taking in the village of Montesanto, and 30 prisoners had been taken. mostly from the 26th Panzer Division. Under cover of the bridgehead 237 Field Company of the Divisional engineers succeeded in bulldozing a crossing of the canal which allowed the 10th Hussars to begin moving across at about 0800 hours. This regiment of the 2nd Armoured Brigade had been under the 56th Division's command until a few days previously, and had only just returned to its parent formation. The Bays having already been deployed with 11 Brigade and the 9th Lancers being held on the leash to go through with the Kangaroo force, 10 H were now allotted the role of armoured support for the Irish Brigade. By mid-morning most of two squadrons had joined the infantry around Montesanto.

Meanwhile B Squadron of the Recce Regiment, with the tanks of the 4th Hussars and the company of Northamptons succeeded in clearing Croatia and so removed a constricting pressure from the right flank. The Surreys, at about the same time, occupied Runco, to the north af the railway and almost up to the Nicolo canal.

In order to obtain a major break-through, however, it was necessary to unleash the Kangaroo force as soon as possible. Before this could be done a larger bridgehead over the Nicolo canal was essential, and 38 Brigade was ordered, therefore, to exploit its gains with all speed.

In spite of stiff opposition and some very heavy shelling, the two Irish battalions succeeded in making a considerable enlargement of the whole bridgehead area by midday, and there was room, at last, for the Kangaroo force to form up over the canal.

This time the orders to the Armoured Brigade were to seize Quartesana and Cona and the bridges over the canals at these two places. The distance involved was about 5 miles from the bridgehead and it was getting late.

After an unpleasant spell in an assembly area, the force began to rattle on its way at about 1500 hours, creeping out into the open through the positions of the Inniskillings. As usual, difficulty was experienced in getting clear of our own forward positions, and before the force was finally in the open it was late in the afternoon.

As they tried to push on, both tanks and infantry came under intense fire from self-propelled guns and enemy tanks. Frequently these were sited in and around the farm buildings which dotted the whole area, and every house was a potential strong point. Several times the infantry were compelled to de-buss and mop up enemy posts of this kind as well as individual enemy with Bazookas who were troublesome over the entire area.

Invaluable assistance to the armour was given by the RAF, whose cab-ranks were at immediate call to the Brigade. A number of enemy strong points, tanks, and guns were destroyed by this means.

As time wore on resistance began to stiffen more and more. Despite all that had been done by the RAF and the infantry in Kangaroos, fire from enemy tanks and self-propelled guns increased. The gunners were trying to give their maximum support, and several "Uncle Targets" were engaged with good effect. It was, however, just beginning to be difficult for the main weight of the divisional artillery to cover the ground ahead of this highly mobile force. It was the first and only occasion during the whole operation when the full weight of the divisional artillery was not available for each portion of the front. Even at this time the armoured force was able to call on the fire of 11 RHA which was moving with the armour, on 17 Field Regiment RA (two batteries using super-charge), and on two medium regiments which were able to give full support).

As darkness began to fall there was a growing atmosphere of suspense. The force, with its tanks and infantry and Kangaroos, was out on its own; no friendly troops were on either flank; close air support was over for the day and gunner support was limited; despite his disorganisation the enemy had plenty of men and guns in the neighbourhood.

Reports kept coming in over the wireless of "Many Krauts on our right", and "Ted transport moving out of range on the left".

A quick conference was held by the 2nd Armoured Brigade's commander: he confirmed that the bridges at Cona and Quartesana were to be seized that night.

The battle which followed was unorthodox, thrilling, and magnificently fruitful. By the light of a bright moon and burning tanks and farm houses, the force approached the bridges simultaneously in two columns. E Company made for Quartesana and F Company for Cona. Chaotic fighting ensued, with tracer flying in every direction.

Quartesana, the approaches to which were continuously under mortar fire, contained three enemy tanks, several strong points of "Bazooka-men", and a number of machine gun posts. The village and the bridge beyond it were rushed by the tanks and Kangaroos and, after knocking out two of the 9th Lancers tanks, the enemy withdrew in confusion into the darkness. The bridge was taken intact.

In Cona a more complex battle developed. An enemy 15cm gun was sited 100 yards beyond the river and was being used to fire over open sights into the area of the bridge and the village. It was backed up by strong groups of machine-gunners and "Bazooka-men". Two attempts were made by F Company, with the tanks, to rush the bridge and the second shot was successful; a firm bridgehead was seized shortly after 2300 hours. and H Company was rushed up to reinforce F Company in holding the ground.

At 0100 hours on the 22nd both bridges were securely in our hands, nearly 10,000 yards beyond the Nicolo Canal which had been the front-line at mid-day. A number of enemy had been killed and nearly 60 prisoners taken. Several trucks and a 15 centimeter gun had been captured: a heavily laden lorry, trying to escape, was hit at close range by a shot from one of our tanks: the cargo was, or had been, artillery ammunition.

Meanwhile other elements of the Division had not been idle. Operating on the right flank of the Armoured Brigade and under its command, 56 Recce Regiment (less B Squadron), advanced during the late afternoon to occupy the general line of the Condito Belriguardo from Voghenza northwards to just short of Quartesana. In the course of this operation many mines and demolitions were encountered and numerous pockets of enemy were eliminated. Voghenza was siezed and 19 prisoners were taken.

At the same time, on the left of the Armoured Brigade, the 36th Brigade with 48 RTR were again doing great things. During the morning of the 21st, while the Irish Brigade was extending its bridgehead over the Nicolo Canal, the Buffs crossed the Fossa di Porto and came up on the left. At 1330 hours the Argylls were put at half an hour's notice to move, and at 1530 hours they, too, were off.

These last few miles before Ferrara covered flat and very open country, which, despite the multitude of canals and dykes, proved to be favourable ground for the tanks. The regiment made the most of it; by 1900 hours, with the Argylls, the armour had reached Possessione San Antonio after encountering resistance similar to that in the Armoured Brigade's sector. Being without Kangaroo Carriers, however, the infantry in this spearhead were less fortunate and suffered a number of casualties, (about 25 wounded), between mid-afternoon and sunset. A number of prisoners was taken, including some ill-mannered Nazis of the 26th Recce Unit.

After nightfall the Argylls, followed now by 6 RWK continued to push on rapidly and by 0100 hours had reached the line of the Po di Volano to the west of Cona. That this was achieved so close on the heels of the Armoured Brigade was a grand success fo the pedestrian infantry.

The Argylls were anxious, having come so far and so rapidly, to push on over the Po di Volano without delay. This request, however, was refused as there were no bridges intact across the river in the sector and tanks would not have been able to follow.

During the small hours of the morning 6 RWK moved round behind the Argylls and began to clear up all the country south of the Po di Volano and as far west as the Divisional boundary, just short of route 16. Just before dawn the peace of Battalion Headquarters in Palmirano was disturbed by the arrival of a German Mark IV tank. Evidently having called on the wrong day it made off in the darkness to try its luck elsewhere. 6 RWK continued clearing up towards the west.

During the same period further moves were taking place in the wake of the 2nd Armoured Brigade's advance. 5 Northamptons were moved up during the night behind the Recce Regiment and took over Voghenza and the line of the Condito Belriguardo. The Recce Regiment, thus relieved, was able to concentrate by first light in Gualdo and the divisions right flank was, at the same time, made firm for the following day. In addition to this relief, 2 LF moved up in the middle of the night and took over Cona from the Armoured Brigade.

During the morning of the 22nd 56 Recce Regiment, still under command of the Armoured Brigade, pushed on towards the Po di Volano in a north-westerly sweep on a broad front from Cona and Quartesana. Enemy infantry were bypassed and useful information was obtained on the state of roads and bridges.

At 1230 hours the Regiment passed to under command of the 11th Brigade, which had, by this time, taken up the lead through the Armoured Brigade's bridgehead.

During the afternoon a good deal of enemy resistance was encountered in the area of Contrapo and thence northwards and eastwards. The Lancashire Fusiliers were directed through the Recce Regiment's positions to try and deal with some of this, and on the right the Northamptons were passed through and directed on the river to the east of the bridge by Fossalta. As evening drew on however, resistance stiffened all along the front and it seemed that a considerable pocket of enemy was contained south of the river between Cona on the left and the Diversivo di Volano, south of Fossalta, on the right.

At the east end of the Diversivo di Volano, which at the time was beyond the Divisional boundary, 167 Brigade of the 56th Division had had a battle in the middle of the day, and little progress had been made from there to the north. Further east, however, in Sabbioncello, the 1st Buffs from the 24th Guards Brigade had crossed the river and found the bridge in an easily reparable state. The main effort of the 56th Division was, therefore, directed on this route.

As a result of this fortunate find the inter-divisional boundary was changed by 5 Corps late on the evening of the 22nd and the main axis of the 78th Division was turned north-east. The 11th Brigade was ordered to take advantage of the presence of the 56th Division on the far side of the river and to establish a bridgehead in the area south of Fossalta. A considerable enemy pocket still remained south of the river, but it had, by evening, been almost entirely compressed into the river bend or "bulge".

During the night the Northamptons crossed the river against negligible opposition, but ran into strong enemy posts almost immediately they began to extend the bridgehead. There was, however, a firm footing on the far side and bridging operations began.

With the exception of the enemy left in the Fossalta bulge, the ground was now clear up to the Po di Volano. From the time at which the 2nd Armoured Brigade and the 36th Infantry Brigade had broken out from the Argenta position, until the 11th Brigade reached and crossed the Po di Volano, was a period of just three days. In this time the enemy had been relentlessly hustled along every inch of his many routes of withdrawal. In the minds of his commanders there must have been a rising panic as the whole force became compressed against the Po's south bank, as the Air Force continued to pound and slash at the crossings of this great river, and as the queues of men and transport, guns, tanks, horses, mules, and all the cumbersome paraphernalia of war, grew larger and thicker in the fields of the plain and along the floodbanks of the river. So long, however, as the line of the Po di Volano held, there was always a chance that another "Dunkirk" might be achieved.

But the line of the Po di Volano had not held; someone had made a tragic bloomer and failed effectively to blow the Sabbioncello bridge; even the limited hope of achieving a "Dunkirk" faded in that second of time.

CHAPTER VII.

Destruction of the enemy south of the river Po.

The morning of April 23rd showed us little major change on our own front, with the Division now closed up to the line of the Po di Valano and the Diversivo di Volano round the Fossalta pocket. 5 Northamptons had a firm bridgehead over the river and the sappers began work on the bridge site at first light.

During the day the Northamptons carried out operations to extend their bridgeheads, and were supported in this by tanks of the Bays which were passed round through the 56th Division's bridgehead in Sabbioncello and thence west along the north bank of the river. At the same time the Lancashire Fusiliers were engaged in trying to wipe out the enemy pocket south of the river by Baura.

By mid-morning the Northamptons succeeded in clearing Fossalta and 11 Brigade was in process of passing the Surreys across the river by boat and raft. Progress everywhere was slow due to the very open country where wide fields of fire were available to the enemy from any of the innumerable little groups of farm-buildings dotted over the plain.

On the right, meanwhile, the 56th Division had made great strides forward and had cleared Copparo by first light. On the left the 8th Indian Division was pushing northwards from the area of Ferrara, and further west a race to the river was in progress. Tanks of the North Irish Horse, (21st Tank Brigade), with the infantry of the 8th Indian Division started to advance at 0600 hours, with the intention of reaching the banks of the river. At 1045 hours they arrived, having taken large numbers of prisoners and bypassed the town of Ferrara altogether. At 1055 hours the 6th Armoured Division's leading tanks reached the Po further to the west, and very shortly afterwards troops of the Fifth Army were reported as being on the south bank at San Benedetto.

On our own front the enemy continued to hold out stubbornly, and at the time it was hard to understand why so little progress was being made towards the river crossings near Polesella.

By evening 1 Surreys were across the river and had joined 5 Northamptons, whilst 56 Recce Regiment with 2 LF were trying to make progress into the area of the "bulge" and to the west of it.

At last light the Northamptons reached Giacomo, at the head of the bulge and the Surreys were beginning to pass through. The bridge was expected to be complete at any time and the Irish Brigade, with the 10th Hussars, was ready to cross over and push on.

At 2300 hours the bridge was ready and 2 Innisks started to cross. The Royal Irish Fusiliers were to follow, and each battalion was supported by tanks of the 10th Hussars.

The plan was as follows. The Brigade would pass through the bridgehead with as little delay as possible, and, with the Inniskillings leading, would seize the village of Saletta. This was chosen as the first Brigade objective because the small village of Tamara, between Fossalta and Saletta, had been occupied during the day by the 1st London Irish Rifles of the 56th Division. Once in Saletta the Inniskillings were to press north directed on the river crossings at Zocca and Ro, whilst the Royal Irish Fusiliers were to strike north-west towards Ruina and the banks of the river west of Zocca.

Having crossed the river the Inniskillings moved north as planned and all went well until they began to approach Saletta at about 0200 hours. Here, in the narrow approaches to the village they began to run into serious trouble. The enemy's determination to stand was not one atom diminished from its earlier intensity, and a fierce battle at close quarters ensued.

At this stage it was becoming glaringly apparent why the approaches to the Po just east of Ferrara were proving so troublesome. The 76th Panzer Corps, containing the 26th Panzer and the 29th Panzer-Grenadier Divisions, which had been given the task of covering the withdrawal of all the other forces, had chosen as its own line of withdrawal the crossings over the Po in the area of Polesella Thanks to the work of the RAF the bulk of this Corps was still waiting to cross.

At 0500 hours on the 24th the fighting in Saletta was over and the Inniskillings were breaking through the town and pushing north. As soon as they were clear of the village the Irish Fusiliers followed and turned towards Ruina. As morning broke both battalions were pushing out slowly but surely towards the Po.

On the left the 11th Brigade with the Bays had also made progress. The Northamptons advancing north-west from Giacomo were nearing Correggio at dawn, and the Surreys, on the right, were preparing to attack a strong enemy position at Corlo, covering the bridge over the canal north-west of the village

During the morning a break began to appear. The Northamptons attacked and captured Correggio; the Surreys forced their way through Corlo and seized the bridge intact — a notable achievement, and one of the first importance at this stage —; the RAF struck at very strong enemy positions on the line of the Canale Fossetta in front of which the Irish Brigade was held up; the Kangaroo force was passed over the river and prepared to strike out on its last task of destruction.

Amidst all this activity a further great work was in hand; plans were being made for crossing the Po and the next stage of the pursuit. In this connection 78th Division had been ordered to cross the river with one brigade group as soon as could be done after reaching the south bank. At the same time, a brigade of the 56th Division was to assault on the right.

The Divisional Commander had chosen the 36th Brigade to lead the Division over the river, and accordingly operations were in progress during the evening of the 23rd and the morning of the 24th to relieve the Brigade of its existing commitments south-east of Ferrara By 1045 hours on the 24th this relief was complete and the 56th Recce Regiment had taken over the Brigade's positions. At mid-day a big planning conference was in progress at Brigade Headquarters; "Fantails" and amphibious tanks were being discussed; the launching and landing beaches were being chosen; a thousand questions, not previously thought of were popping up to puzzle; and at 1300 hours the operation was cancelled. The 6th Armoured, 2nd New Zealand and 8th Indian Divisions were all up to the Po further to the west, and were meeting no opposition on the banks: it was obviously a waste of time for bridging operations to be delayed until the 78th Division reached the river through an area still strongly held by the enemy.

Soon after mid-day the 2nd Armoured Brigade's private army was launched. It was ordered to pass between the two infantry brigades and sweep westwards towards the Ferrara — Pontelagoscuro canal, moving between the Canale Fossetta and the Fossa Lavezzola.

At the same time the 11th Brigade was to do a similar sweep westwards and clear the ground between the Canale Fossetta and the Po di Volano.

The Irish Brigade was to continue on its original axis, directed on Zocca and Ruina.

"Mobile battles" and "fluid situations" reigned during the afternoon, but as evening approached a distinct stiffening of resistance was noticeable on the Armoured Brigade's front. At 1800 hours there were reports of many enemy tanks in the area just north of Ferrara, and shortly afterwards, as the light was failing, the 9th Lancers fought an exciting action in which 7 enemy Mark IV tanks, moving north-east towards the ferries, were knocked aus for the loss of only one of their own.

By this time a peculiar state of affairs had been reached. Having swept right across the 11th Brigade's front, the Kangaroo force was strung out for some 4,000 yards with an open right flank and with tank-actions in progress over the whole area; night was drawing on; the infantry,in their Kangaroos, were a wonderful target for lurking enemy tanks in the general confusion and semi-darkness. To exploit the enemy's distress, however, it was decided that the battle would be pressed on by moonlight. The landscape was ablaze with burning houses and vehicles: further north the RAF was dropping flares and bombing the roads and railways beyond the Po: in addition to the fires caused by bombing, shelling and mortaring, a new destruction had begun — the enemy was setting light to everything he had.

At 2030 hours 5 Corps telephoned to say there were strong indications that the enemy had lost control of the situation. Intelligence channels had intercepted messages from the German command that the situation was desperate, and that each man must fend for himself. It was believed that the chief confusion was centered around the river-crossings north of Pescara and Francolino.

As a result of this information the Divisional Commander ordered the 2nd Armoured Brigade to swing round to the north, cross the Fossa Lavezzola and make for the "disorderly enemy". This was not, however, to be done before the engagement already in progress was brought to an end.

At 2235 hours the Armoured Brigade, having had some four hours of intense and swift fighting, reported that things were beginning to quieten down. There had been a great deal of hostile fire from enemy tanks and self-propelled guns throughout the Brigade battle zone and the force had become widely dispersed, each portion, including Brigade Headquarters, having had its own battle to fight. The intention was now to collect the bits and pieces together and move on towards the river as soon as possible.

In order to carry out this new task and switch the axis through more than ninety degrees, a deliberate advance was decided upon and a fire plan was arranged By 0130 hours the infantry with F and G Companies up, began to feel their way north, the tanks following some distance behind, ready to press through if opposition was met.

In the past few hours, however, the whole complexion of the front had changed. At sunset on the 24th there had been strong groups of enemy tanks and self-propelled guns mingled with numerous small detachments of infantry equipped with machine guns and bazookas. These forces- although scattered and dis-organised, had known their job and were determined to do it. They were to delay our advance by every means at their disposal, and especially in front of the crossings at Polesella, Zocca and Francolino. They were to fight until all their main elements had crossed the river.

As dawn approached on the 25th this was no longer the case. Organised resistance was at an end.

A plan made overnight for the swift and thorough clearance of the whole divisional area was put into effect at first light. One squadron of the Recce Regiment passed to under command of each of the 11th, 38th and 2nd Armoured Brigades, and these three formations were each given an area stretching south from a sector of the river bank.

On the right the Irish Brigade entered Zocca and Ruina to find an incredible scene of devastation. Packed in the fields, queued up in lanes, cast in ditches, in farmyards and woods, everywhere — even in the river itself — lay the remains of the transport and equipment of the 76th Panzer Corps. Practically everything was destroyed: anything that had not been riddled with cannon — shell or torn by bomb splinters from the air forces, had been burnt by the enemy as he fled. The only large quantity of serviceable things seemed to be the horses; these, abandoned, roamed everywhere amongst the devastation.

To the west of Ruina the 11th Brigade was given a sector to clear up to the river, and here similar conditions prevailed, although there was less equipment than in the Irish Brigade's area. Having cleared up to the bank by mid-day the task of watching the river was handed over the Recce Squadron and the battalions concentrated in Baura (2 LF), Corlo (1 Surreys), and Correggio (5 Northamptons).

On the left of the divisional sector the 2nd Armoured Brigade did similar sweeping up and also handed over the river line to the Recce Squadron by evening.

The story is over; the intention of the Allied Armies in Italy was carried through to the end; on the ground before us was evidence enough of how much our enemy had lost. Despite all, however, few realised how near this was to the end, not of a phase in the war, but of the whole odious epoch. One of those who knew was Lieutenant General Graf von Schwerin commander of the 76th Panzer Corps who, with his personal staff, surrendered to the 27th Lancers on the morning of April 25th. On being asked the dispositions of his Corps a that time, he is said to have replied — "You will find it south of the River Po".

No small part of this vast achievement was due to the Air Forces: the accuracy of their bombing and fire, the promptness of their action on receiving a request, and, best of all, their constant presence in the air above our heads — all these things hastened victory more than any can tell. No small part was played by each of the other divisions which fought in the fight. In this report, however, we set out to describe the actions of our own division; its part was not a small one either.

TABLE I.

Casualties of the 78th Division 9th to 25th April 1945.

The table shows casualties by units under headings X (killed), Y (wounded), Z (missing), for the following periods:

9 — 11 April: Preliminary operations.

12 — 15 April: From the Santerno to the Reno.

16 — 18 April: Breaking the Argenta Gap.

19 — 22 April: From after Argenta to the Po di Volano.

23 — 25 April: Final closing to the banks of the Po.

TABLE I

Casualties of 11 Brit Inf Bde 9th to 25th April, 1945.

Formations and Units.		Dates in April 1945																		
		9 – 11			12 – 15			16 – 18			19 – 22			23 – 25			Total 9 – 25 April			
		X	Y	Z	X	Y	Z	X	Y	Z	X	Y	Z	X	Y	Z	X	Y	Z	X+Y+Z
2 L. F.	Offrs	1	2						2		2	2					3	6		9
	OR	3	24					2	13		3	18			6		8	61		69
	Total	4	26					2	15		5	20			6		11	67		78
1 Surreys	Offrs										1				1		1	1		2
	OR		3					2	18		5	14		5	10		12	45		57
	Total		3					2	18		6	14		5	11		13	46		59
5 Northamptons	Offrs	1							1			1			1		1	.3		4
	OR		5					3	20		2	24		2	8		7	57		64
	Total	1	5					3	21		2	25		2	9		8	60		68
Total 11 Brigade	Offrs	2	2						3		3	3			2		5	10		15
	OR	3	32					7	51		10	56		7	26		27	165		192
	Total	5	34					7	54		13	59		7	28		32	175		207

TABLE I (Cont)

Casualties of 36 Inf Bde
9th to 25th April, 1945.

Formations and Units.		9 – 11			12 – 15			16 – 18			19 – 22			23 – 25			Total 9 – 25 April			
		X	Y	Z	X	Y	Z	X	Y	Z	X	Y	Z	X	Y	Z	X	Y	Z	X+Y+Z
5 Buffs	Offrs	1	2						2			2					1	6		7
	OR	1	14		2	1			9		5	21					8	45		53
	Total	2	16		2	1			11		5	23					9	51		60
6 R.W.K.	Offrs				1	1						2					1	3		4
	OR				5	16			3		5	10			2		10	31		41
	Total				6	17			3		5	12			2		11	34		45
8 A. & SH.	Offrs					1					2	1					2	2		4
	OR		4		3	6					16	45		1	7		20	62		82
	Total		4		3	7					18	46		1	7		22	64		86
Total 36 Brigade	Offrs	1	2		1	2			2		2	5					4	11		15
	OR	1	18		10	23			12		26	76		1	9		38	138		176
	Total	2	20		11	25			14		28	81		1	9		42	149		191

TABLE I (Cont)

Casualties of 38 (Irish) Inf Bde 9th to 25th April, 1945.

Formations and Units.		\multicolumn{21}{c}{Dates in April 1945}																			
		9 – 11			12 – 15			16 – 18			19 – 22			23 – 25			Total 9 - 25 April			
		X	Y	Z	X	Y	Z	X	Y	Z	X	Y	Z	X	Y	Z	X	Y	Z	X+Y+Z
2 Innisks	Offrs					1						4			3			8		8
	OR				2	6		5	26		17	53	1	4	21	1	28	106	2	136
	Total				2	7		5	26		17	57	1	4	24	1	28	114	2	144
2 L. I. R.	Offrs									1		3						3	1	4
	OR				1	10			2	33	3	44			6	1	4	62	34	100
	Total				1	10			2	34	3	47			6	1	4	65	35	104
1 R. I. F.	Offrs								2						2			4		4
	OR					2		3	21		6	14			1		9	38		47
	Total					2		3	23		6	14			3		9	42		51
Total 38 Brigade	Offrs					1			2	1		7			5	1		15	1	16
	OR				3	18		8	49	33	26	111	1	4	28	2	41	206	36	283
	Total				3	19		8	51	34	26	118	1	4	33	2	41	221	37	299

TABLE I (Cont)

Casualties of R. A. 78th Division

9th to 25th April, 1945.

Formations and Units.		9 – 11			12 – 15			16 – 18			19 – 22			23 – 25			Total 9 = 25 April			
		X	Y	Z	X	Y	Z	X	Y	Z	X	Y	Z	X	Y	Z	X	Y	Z	t+Y+7
17 Field Regiment	Offrs																	2		2
	OR											1		1	8		1	9		10
	Total											1		1	8		1	11		12
132 Field Regiment	Offrs																			
	OR													1	1		1	1		1
	Total													1	1		1	1		2
138 Field Regiment	Offrs																			
	OR		1			1					1	1					1	2		3
	Total		1			1					1	1					1	3		4
64. Anti-Tank Regiment	Offrs																	1		1
	OR										1	5			4		1	9		10
	Total										1	6			4		1	10		11
Total Divisional Artillery	Offrs					1						3		1			1	4		5
	OR		1								2	7		1	13		3	21		24
	Total		1			1					2	10		2	13		4	25		29

TABLE I (Cont)

Casualties of Remainder of 78th Division 9th to 25th April, 1945.

Formations and Units.		9 – 11			12 – 15			16 – 18			19 – 23			23 – 25			Total 9 – 25 April			
		X	Y	Z	X	Y	Z	X	Y	Z	X	Y	Z	X	Y	Z	X	Y	Z	X+Y+Z
56 Recce Regiment	Offrs										1	2					1	2		3
	OR		3		3						3	8			4		6	15		21
	Total		3		3						4	10			4		7	17		24
R. E.	Offrs											1						1		1
	OR		2			2						2						6		6
	Total		2			2						3						7		7
Divisional Signals	Offrs																			
	OR											6						6		6
	Total											6						6		6
1 Kensingtons	Offrs														1			1		1
	OR														1			1		1
	Total																			
R. A. M. C.	Offrs										1						1			
	OR										1	2					1	2		3
	Total										1	2					1	2		3
Provost	Offrs																			
	OR											1						1		1
	Total											1						1		1
Divisional Headquarters	Offrs											1						1		1
	OR										1	3					1	3		4
	Total										1	4					1	4		5

TABLE I (Cont)

Total Casualties of 78th Division 9th to 25th April, 1945.

	Dates in April 1945																	
	9 – 11			12 – 15			16 – 18			19 – 22			23 – 25			Total 9 – 25 April			
	X	Y	Z	X	Y	Z	X	Y	Z	X	Y	Z	X	Y	Z	X	Y	Z	X+Y+Z
Oftrs	3	4		1	4			7		6	22		1	7		11	44	1	56
OR	4	56		16	43		15	112	33	69	272	1	13	81	2	117	564	36	717
Total	7	60		17	47		15	119	34	75	294	1	14	88	2	128	608	37	773

TABLE II.

Prisoners of War taken by 78th Division

9th to 25th April 1945.

The table shows totals of prisoners which passed through the Divisional Prisoner of War cage for the following periods: —

- 9 — 11 April: Preliminary operations.
- 12 — 15 April: From R. Santerno to R. Reno.
- 16 — 18 April: Argenta.
- 19 — 22 April: From Argenta to the Po di Volano.
- 23 — 25 April: From the Po di Volano to the Po.

Period	Offrs	OR	Total
9 — 11 April	—	32	32
12 — 15 April	2	546	548
16 — 18 April	4	505	509
19 — 22 April	26	1287	1313
23 — 25 April	15	787	802
Total 9 — 25 April	47	3157	3204

PART TWO

Unit Accounts

11 Brigade at Argenta Gap

11 Brigade Headquarters
(See Map V)

Introduction

The mine strewn beaches of Anzio and Salerno Bay, the mountain winter lines along the icy Sangro and snowy Appenines, the "impregnable" Gothic Line, even the formidable Cassino Fortress itself were not to be compared for one moment with this superbly situated and ingeniously exploited strategical strong point that the Brigade was destined to attack during that month of April 1945.

Such were the impressions we gained from the available reports on the notorious "Gap" at Argenta, and even sitting on the floodbanks of the Senio two weeks before the Spring offensive of 1945 started it was obvious that these impressions were not over-exaggerated. The probability that 11 Brigade would have to storm this vital point of the German defences in Italy was taken into account in the pre-offensive planning so it was with eager personal interest that we studied maps and photographs of the area. From the maps it was apparent the position would be ideal for defence, from the air photographs it looked impossible of penetration. The natural barriers were considerable, the "improvements" carried out by the cunning enemy left one with but a single choice for direction of attack. To the north and east of Argenta lay the "Bonifica di Argenta", formerly part of the extensive Valli di Commachio which had been drained of water by endless patient toil and with the aid of expensive modern machinery. This area had become prosperous fertile farm-land with numerous flourishing steadings controlling vast tracts of first class yielding soil. All this had been destroyed entirely by the enemy with typical Teutonic thoroughness — the dams and dykes were breached, the pumping stations smashed and the entire area re-flooded leaving only the tops of the houses and the forlorn white streak of Route 16 on its high embankment, visible in all the watery desolation.

Similar measures and similar results existed to the South and West of Argenta town — here if possible the position was worse as the swamps and naturally waterlogged ground stretched to within 15 Km of Bologna itself and in addition the Reno River with its towering floodbanks provided an effective tank-proof obstacle for any attack originating from the West.

The gap between these two watery barriers consisted of a narrow funnel of dry land averaging 2½ miles in width throughout its length of 5 miles, based on the town of Argenta itself. Inside this restricted area the enemy had carefully built up his long planned defences to perfection. It was proved during subsequent operations that work on these defences had commenced as long before as the summer of 1943 and no pains had been spared to ensure that the soldiers defending the area would be provided with every possible chance of success. Each ditch and canal had been dug out on the Southern side and methodically fortified with strongly revetted positions, numerous OP and HQ sites had been recced and earmarked, every culvert and bridge was prepared for demolition, even booby traps were laid in position and sealed off. But most fantastic of all were the minefields — indeed the whole gap was one single solid minefield — never before had we encountered such a concentrated piece of mining — in shape the main field was triangular, with its apex at Bastia and stretching East for a distance of more than 3 miles. The mines here had been laid in peace conditions and the ground had since lain fallow — much to the annoyance of the surrounding Italian farmers. The mined areas were now completely overgrown and it was quite impossible to pick out the dangerous places. Before the offensive, however, a great stroke of luck, resulted in information being obtained from partisans as to the exact situation of the safe paths through this field, which contributed enormously to the success of the battles to come.

To the North lay further scattered fields between the Reno and the water to the East as far as the Fossa Marina — a 12ft wide waterway running diagonally across the Northern end of the Gap and constituting the most formidable continuous natural obstacle in the bottleneck.

So much for the Argenta Gap itself — now what was the reason for all the special attention in this particular part of the Italian countryside? Surely, if necessary, the main direction of attack from the South could completely by-pass Argenta to the West, further up the Po Valley, therefore why was there this need for special preparation?

The answer was this. — The most important factor at stake during the battles South of the Po was to cut off and capture as many of the enemy as possible before they could cross the river Po and escape to the North. If Argenta was not attacked and the main drive put in to the West it would have to be so much farther West as to allow the enemy unrestricted access to first class Po crossing such as Pontelagoscuro north of Ferrara and others equally good to the East. The enemy would probably be able to ferry over sufficient troops to organise resistance farther North perhaps along the shortened line of the Adige and so delay our further progress more than was desired. Argenta had to be forced by attackers to get at the Ferrara Po crossings quickly and accordingly the enemy appreciated that a firm stand here was absolutely essential to allow the 10 and 14 Armies access to some of their main escape routes to the North. The proviso was that sufficient troops must be made available immediately after the opening of a Po offensive to man the Argenta defences. It was here that the enemy made his big mistke, in leaving too late the commitment of his reserve forces to the area — which enabled the Gap to be broken and the river crossings secured with consequent chaotic results for 76 Pz Corps in particular — but all this was not accomplished without a hard and bloody struggle.

Crossing the Reno and moving up to the mouth of the Gap.

At 0330 hours on the 15th April the new Bailey bridge over the R Reno was proclaimed in working order. The Brigade crossed with the Surreys in the lead. At 1100 hours just as the Surreys were ready to pass through 167 Brigade of 56 Division the first counter-order arrived. 11 Brigade was to switch its axis to pass through 169 Brigade to the North. So it was not until dusk that the Surreys moved up through the 2/7 Queens into the mouth of the Argenta Gap. Acting simultaneously with the Surreys, the Northamptons to the West passed through the left flanking positions of the Queens and were soon moving parallel between the Reno and the railway. During the 16th two tenacious strongholds on the Northampton's front (in the area of Celetta) were summarily dealt with in a perfect example of infantry — aircraft cooperation. Fighter bombers were called in to help and six very bomb happy survivors of their attention were eloquent witnesses of the severely accurate bombing and strafing that resulted. Fifty PW were taken that day. Four or five were from the crack 29 Panzer Grenadier Division: the information they gave was of the highest significance. Their division had recently moved in a very great hurry out of the battles NE of Bologna across the Po and had been directed to the Adige river defences farther North. Apparently a sudden last minute change in plans had resulted in a switch round of the Grenadier battalions to the South with orders to stem the flood at Argenta at all costs. The tanks of the Division were mainly left North of the Po, but the motorised infantry troops (some of the finest the Wehrmacht had produced) were now being recommited, almost too late, opposite 11 Brigade This step was a sure indication that the enemy were at last realising their mistake and appreciating fully the significance of our drive through the gap — this was proof positive the battle to come would be a hard and bloody one, with no quarter asked for or given.

By last light on the 16th the stiffening of the front was obvious. The Northamptons on the left were right up to Argenta cemetery on the Southern outskirts of the town with patrols probing forward to test the enemy defences — which were proved to be especially strong at the station and surrounding buildings. On the right the Surreys were beginning to outflank the town from the North and were moving up to the Fossa Marina, the 12ft wide transverse tank proof obstacle which the enemy had chosen for his all out stand. This was the last and most difficult natural obstacle in the Gap itself, nearly everywhere we were now through the worst mined areas and if our advance was not stopped here it would be the beginning of the end for the enemy. At dusk forward movement was temporarily halted as the Brigade Commander made his plan for the attack over the Fossa Marina. That this attack would have to be carried out by fresh troops on a battalion scale was a foregone conclusion and the Lancashire Fusiliers, until then in Brigade reserve, were quickly moved up and concentrated just behind the leading companies of the Surreys, from which position they would be favourably situated to spring off and penetrate the Marina line.

The attack over the Fossa Marina and the final stages.

The line of the canal was held by II and III battalions of 71 Panzer Grenadier Regiment of 29 Panzer Grenadier Division — two of the hardest fighting units then at the disposal of the German Commander in Italy. For support they had approximately twenty to thirty self propelled and tank destroyer equipments and the usual artillery and mortar sub-units from Regiment and Divisional resources. To attack them was the single infantry battalion of the Lancashire Fusiliers, backed up by the supporting arms already enumerated. 2100 hours was set as H-hour and exactly on the dot the barrage opened with a soul — shattering roar that seemed to shake the very atmosphere itself and lit up the flat surrounding farmland as if it were day. The vital consequences of the barrage were only discovered after the battle, when it was proved that the enemy had been surprised in the middle of a relief and many troops who were moving up to the trenches were caught in the open without cover and as a result suffered disastrous casualties, which affected subsequent operations.

As the barrage opened, the Surreys' leading companies moved nearer to the canal banks and from their firmly established bases the Lancashire Fusiliers sprang forward at the main defences. Within twenty minutes the Fusiliers were engaged in fierce hand to hand fighting with the fanatically resisting enemy — the fury of the struggle continuing unabated for nearly forty minutes. By 2200 hours however, it became evident that the terrific vigour of the attack was beginning to take effect and shortly after the news came through that one infantry company was across complete and in process of beating off a series of hastily organised counter attacks. A second company forced its way over the waterway within another hour and soon the familiar signs of disintegration among the enemy ranks began to show themselves. Over forty PW had been taken and more were coming in every minute — hundreds of dead were counted on the far banks and floating in the blood soaked waters of the canal itself.

Three of the Bays tanks had by this time also succeeded in crossing the canal by means of superhuman efforts on the part of an Ark tank and the supporting Royal Engineers who had established a serviceable bridge immediately behind the first infantry company to cross the canal, approximately 2 Km NE of Argenta town.

The bridgehead won by midnight then was two companies strong and in depth measured nearly three hundred yards constituting a menacing salient right into the crust of the enemy fortress. Three strong counter attacks had been successfully beaten off and not an inch ceded to the enemy. At this stage however, the bridgehead troops were pinned to ground by an accurate and devastating counter barrage which the enemy kept up for the remainder of that night. The Battalion Commander Lt-Col. M. C. Pulford. MC, had unfortunately been woundet in the initial stages of the attack and Major J. A. H. Saunders, 2 i/c, took over for the rest of the battle — fighting the battalion with great courage and skill which later won for him the award of the D.S.O.

When dawn broke the fatal breach in the enemy line was still there and the road lay open for fresh troops to get at the vital inner defences. The enemy's flanks too were beginning to show signs of wavering and taking advantage of this the Surreys quickly moved up a company on the left of the Lancashire Fusiliers to occupy the North Eastern outskirts of Argenta itself.

The town, however, was still held strongly by part of III/71 Panzer Grenadier Regiment as was proved by patrols from the Northamptons which had attempted to infiltrate during the night.

But the main doors had been forced open, and that morning the Irish Fusiliers and the Inniskillings were passed through. At 1700 hours on the 17th the Northamptons began the unenviable task of clearing up the enemy pockets in Argenta itself and three hours later were in full occupation They found that their worst problem was the disposal of the numerous civilian dead who lay piled in gruesome masses, mute testimony to the previous artillery and air bombardment which had reduced the town to heaps of shattered rubble.

Trapped between the Northamptons in Argenta and the Inniskillings to the North, the Germans put in a counter-attack, on the left forward company of the Northamptons. The attack was broken up by sustained fire from our infantry and gunners and the remnants of the attacking force were taken prisoner. The much-vaunted defences of the Gap had been irreparably smashed and the numerically superior enemy so knocked about that the remainder of that regiment of 29 Division was never again able to fight as an effective unit.

The Battle of Argenta

(See Map V).

5th Battalion The Northamptonshire Regiment.

On the morning of Sunday 15th April 1945 the Battalion moved to a concentration area at Castelletto, some 6,000 metres East of Bastia. Companies were warned to be ready for committal the following day, and the men settled down to a day's rest, some basking in the bright sunlight, others chasing guinea fowl in the hopes of an appetising supper. The Padre held a Church Service in a field close by at about 4 o'clock in the afternoon. At Battalion Headquarters the Commanding Officer was unable to issue orders owing to the constant changes of plan. Finally, at 2250 hours whilst orders were being issued to Company Commanders for an operation to take place on Monday, 16th April, in support of the 1st Surreys, the Brigadier phoned up giving orders for an immediate advance to be made by the Battalion on Argenta, between the River Reno and the railway line to Portomaggiore, a frontage of about two miles: the Battalion was to capture Argenta, if possible, but was not to become involved, and if opposition became stiff then close contact with the enemy was to be kept and advantage taken of any weakness that might develop. Little information as to the enemy dispositions or the disposition of the London Scottish about Bastia was available. It was known, however, that over about half of the 4,000 yards advance to Argenta, extensive minefields existed. The ground was flat, but covered with orchards, vineyards and scattered trees, with on the left flank the flood bank of the Reno rising 15 feet, affording ample cover for enemy snipers and MG posts. The ground could not be reconnoitred, but excellent aerial photographs were distributed down to company level.

Fresh orders were immediately issued, based on a simple plan — a controlled advance on a three company front by bounds.

The advance started about 0245 hours on Monday 16th April, the order of battle being — "D" Company right, moving along railway line, "B" Company centre, "A" Company on the left on Route 16, and clearing the Reno floodbank, and "C" Company in reserve.

"A" Company moved rapidly along the road and river bank for about 1.500 yards, where strong opposition was met on the edge of the main minefield, and from beyond the Reno. When this opposition was finally overcome, "A" Company became the reserve Company, providing left flank protection.

"B" Company in the centre moved more slowly across open country, and just before dawn, after an advance of about 1,700 yards, came up against strong opposition covering the southern exits to the main minefield. Fortunately at first light tanks and flail tanks reached the Battalion, and though delayed by bridges breaking, managed to support "B" Company quickly. However, it was not until fighter bombers assisted that the opposition was finally cleared. "B" Company now pushed on up Route 16 towards Argenta. It was only possible to move on a very narrow front, on account of the thick minefields which existed on each side of the road. It was an easy matter for the enemy to concentrate on the narrow northern exit of the minefield, and "B" Company was unable to progress further than 100 yards from this exit, as the flail tanks were withdrawn and could not clear mines to assist the company to manoeuvre.

"D" Company on the right advanced slowly, meeting isolated opposition, until finally held at the S. E. outskirts of the town at about 1615 hours on Monday, 16th April.

"C" Company, in reserve, mopped up the area of the advance, capturing numerous prisoners.

Tac HQ moved up to a more central position during the evening of 16th April.

During the night 16th — 17th April "B" Company kept the attention of the enemy drawn to the South, whilst "D" Company made efforts to enter the town from the East. These efforts were unsuccessful, the opposition which was met showing that the enemy was fully determined to contest the town. The following morning, Tuesday 17th April, the enemy attempted to infiltrate into "D" Company's area, but were destroyed. This greatly improved the position. "D" Company was able to advance and capture the cemetery — a strategic point commanding the S. E. entrance of Argenta.

At about mid-day on Tuesday 17th April, definite orders were received to attack and capture Argenta at all costs. Owing to the minefields a more complicated plan became necessary. "C" Company was to advance on the East of the railway line to Argenta railway station, then turn left and attack the town. In support of the attack was air bombardment, a squadron of 'Crocodiles' and a troop of Churchills. The general plan was to take the town sector by sector, one company passing through another.

At 1730 hours 17th April, a heavy artillery concentration was brought down on the town, and "C" Company crossed the start line. Wireless communication had been established with both Churchills and Crocodiles down to a platoon-troop level, and was found to work extremely well throughout the operation.

"C" Company's first objective was the railway station, and here the leading platoon established itself and consolidated, with the Churchills in support. No. 13 Platoon went straight through and cleared the right-hand portion of the town, their Crocodiles flaming all likely points of resistance as well as all actual ones. The operation was going well, and resistance had proved less difficult than had been anticipated, and the third platoon passed through the first sector and cleared the left-hand portion. From then on opposition was small, and the few remaining resisters were neutralised with the aid of the Crocodiles.

Owing to the small resistance it was decided to push "C" Company on through the town, and by 2000 hours the company was established at the fork road, covering the main entrance into the town from the north-west — Route 16. The remainder of the Battalion quickly followed up and Battalion HQ was established in the town, all companies consolidating the positions gained.

First warning of a counter-attack came at 0230 hours 18th April, with brisk exchanges of Bren and Spandau fire followed by the crack of an 88 gun from an enemy tank which rolled down the road through "C" Company's leading platoon lines until halted by a P.I.A.T. shot when sitting right on the fork roads. Enemy infantry were infiltrating round the flanks and along the banks of the Reno, and some close and fierce hand-to-hand battles were fought in the darkness. DFs were brought down by artillery and the Battalion Mortars, who by putting in extra secondaries were firing 200 yards beyond their maximum range. In "C" Company's area a fierce battle raged and an attempt by enemy infantry to probe down Route 16 into the town was stopped, the enemy retiring, leaving dead behind. A second enemy tank which had lain back up Route 16 added to the confusion with some low and accurate fire from its heavy gun. Counter-attacks were launched by "C" Company and after fierce hand-to-hand struggles and grenade exchanges the enemy tanks retired, one in a damaged condition.

A second attempt to break down our defence was made with support from the second tank, but this met with even less success than the first, and by 0400 hours the enemy finally withdrew, leaving his dead and large quantities of arms, ammunition and equipment behind.

Heavy shelling into the town had broken all line communications, but wireless worked splendidly and Battalion signallers were busy all night under shell fire repairing the lines.

Daylight found our positions intact, the situation which had been severely contested perfectly secure, and troops of 36 Brigade moving round on our right flank to cut off Route 16 away to the north-west of the town.

The battle for, and leading up to, Lungurella.

(See map VI).

1st Battalion the East Surrey Regiment.

The battle for, and leading up to Lungurella started for The 1st Battalion The East Surrey Regiment when they had left Consandolo in TCVs for a forward concentration area near Ripapersico arriving there about 2245 hours on 19th April 1945.

The Brigade plan for this action was for the 2 LF, followed by the 1st East Surreys to pass through the bridgehead over the Fossa di Porto. 2 LF were to strike westwards, and the East Surreys northwards through Runco to Lungurella

The present state of enemy opposition was stated to be light and disorganised. This report, however, proved to be quite groundless as will be seen from the bitter fighting which took place before the Battalion succeeded in entering Lungurella a little over two days later.

At about 0245 hours on the 20th April the Battalion left their concentration area by march route but, due to the difficulties encountered by the 2 LF, were two hours late in crossing the Fossa di Porto. The order of march was "A" Company, followed by "B" and "D" Companies, with "C" Company in reserve. When dawn broke Tac HQ and "C" Company were established over the canal, but the rifle companies found themselves a little to the North and feeling extremely naked.

That morning was memorable for "B" Company, for shortly after first light, having taken up a position round a cluster of farm buildings about 100 yards in the rear of "A" Company, a heavy mortar bomb exploded on the roof of the barn where breakfast was being served. Fortunately most of the Company had already eaten their breakfast and there was only one casualty.

The Battalion was unable to continue its advance as 2 LF were encountering stiff resistance from the area of Il Quartiere in the form of sniper and MG fire.

Lt Col HMA Hunter, MBE, who was commanding the Battalion, then formulated the plan of attacking in a northerly direction, thereby bypassing the resistance to the East.

"C" Company was to secure a bridgehead over the railway running North-West from Portomaggiore and "D" Company was to move up on the right and secure the road junction on the Runco — Portomaggiore road. This attack was to be preceded by the Wasps in attacking a group of houses, just to the North of the start line where it was suspected that there might be an enemy strongpoint.

At 1015 hours the Wasps reported their objective cleared, and immediately afterwards "C" and "D" Companies commenced their advance. "C" Company, under the command of Major EH Giles, MC, moving forward in open formation, secured their bridgehead and were soon joined by "D" Company. During the advance both Companies were being continually harassed by snipers and AP shells that were being directed at the supporting tanks, but no casualties were inflicted.

Whilst exploiting forward from the bridgehead 13 Platoon was ordered to attack a house on the right of the Company's axis of advance from which heavy fire was coming. 14 Platoon were working round to a position to give them covering fire when all three Bren gunners were killed and Sgt Charlton seriously wounded. However he led 14 Platoon on to a position from which they could support 13 Platoon and the objective was captured.

Throughout the morning the Battalion continued its advance with "D" Company right and "C" Company left, but soon the position became very confused owing to the fact that Company Commanders were unable to say exactly where they were due to the regular pattern of the ground which was very flat with continual drainage ditches running at regular intervals across the axis of advance. From the banks of these drainage ditches the enemy were harassing our troops with both sniper and Spandau fire. The position during the afternoon became even more confused with the conflicting reports as to the positions of the forward troops.

At about 1500 hours, "C" Company, was forced to cede some of the ground it had gained during the morning, due to a heavy enemy DF that was brought down in the area of their leading troops and, as they were withdrawing to take cover in a ditch some fifty yards to their rear, were enfiladed by small arms fire which inflicted several casualties. They were then counter-attacked under cover of the enemy barrage, and were again forced back to the ditch immediately to their rear.

It was during this counter attack that Lieut JF Louis the platoon commander with the longest record of service with the Battalion, having joined the Battalion in North Africa in December 1942 — was killed by a burst of Spandau fire. Lieut Louis was unfortunately not the only casualty, and L Cpl Morrish found that he was the only NCO present that still survived. He immediately assumed command of the platoon, although himself wounded, and rallying the platoon, led a counter attack which completely caught the enemy unawares and enabled the company to continue their advance and capture Gobbia, their objective.

"D" Company was experiencing similar trouble. for they found themselves pinned down in a ditch by ever increasing small arms fire. The leading Platoon

Commanders, Lieut JWC Ledger of 17 Platoon and Lieut FGM Keiger of 18 Platoon being unable to contact their Company HQ as the 38 Set had been put out of action, decided in conjunction with the tank commander that it was still possible to gain their final objective by covering the tanks forward in bounds. However, the leading tank got bogged in spite of using a Fascine and whilst the other tank attempted to tow the first one out both were bazookad and set on fire forcing the crews to abandon their tanks and join the infantry in the ditch.

Then a heavy enemy stonk came down in the area — forcing both platoons to retire. At this stage Major CP Genillard, MC, who commanded the company, arrived on the scene, having crawled forward alone under intense small arms fire. He proceeded to make a plan whereby 17 platoon was to return to the position it had just vacated and support 18 platoon on to the final objective. Here 17 platoon came up against some unexpected trouble, for it was found that a party of some ten to twenty Boche had crept forward under cover of the stonk and were occupying the ditch which 17 platoon had just left. Major CP Genillard, MC, was then forced to withdraw 17 and 18 platoons to the East to join 16 platoon. This was accomplished under cover of smoke.

The casualties suffered by "C" and "D" Companies during the afternoon were — "C" Company, Lieut JF Louis and four ORs killed and nine wounded and "D" Company three ORs killed and one wounded.

During the day "C" and "D" Companies had taken sixty five prisoners, quite apart from the many that had been killed. They were a strangely assorted collection, including many new identifications from 155 Division — a training and garrison division — never before committed in battle and only recently brought South of the Po to bolster up the morale of the seriously mauled Panzer Grenadiers. One prisoner was even dressed in civilian clothes, explaining himself by saying that he had been hiding for five days and was too frightened to attempt to escape in uniform.

At 2030 hours "A" and "B" Companies relieved "D" and "C" Companies. By 2130 hours they had attacked and captured Gobbietta and some farm buildings two to three hundred yards East of it.

Shortly before dawn, No. 10 Platoon, commanded by Lieut LAS Harbourne, MC, was ordered forward to sieze and hold a canal crossing North of the railway. The Platoon, which was accompanied by Capt Booth, FOO of 132 Field Regiment, RA., succeeded in occupying a farmhouse some eight hundred yards South of the canal, but was unable to proceed any further. Later in the day, after the platoon had moved on, the roof of this house collapsed killing some gunners who had only recently moved in.

No. 16 Platoon, "D" Company, with one tank in support had in the meanwhile gone through on the right flank, and had by 0500 hours on the 21st, without incident, advanced through Runco to within 150 yards of the canal running South of Lungurella. By 0700 hours, 16 Platoon was joined by the rest of the Company. It was obvious that the enemy had not expected such a rapid advance, for on the approach of daylight a number of enemy could be seen furiously digging in on the opposite bank of the canal. Quick advantage of this was taken both by L Cpl McNally of the Sniper Section, attached to "D" Company, and the two forward platoons, for when the Battalion eventually crossed the canal, four dead Boche were found all shot through the centre of the forehead.

It was not possible for "D" Company to get any nearer to the canal, for whenever they left their cover they were met by heavy and accurate DF and Spandau fire. They were unable to see, however, whether the all important bridge over the canal leading to Lungurella was still intact. The enemy seemed to realise the importance of holding this bridge.

TAC HQ, together with Main HQ, was established in an excellent building to the North of Gobbietta. The only trouble about this house was that there was a dead horse in one of the downstairs room. How it had ever got through the small door into the room will always remain a mystery. However, due to the possibility of Brigade HQ taking over the house it was decided not to try to remove the swollen and already stinking carcass.

During the morning, "B" Company with 12 Platoon leading — commanded by Lieut RR McLean — had been edging forward over open country, under every conceivable type of DF fire, and had succeeded in occupying a large farm some four hundred yards to the South of the canal. At the farm were found nearly one hundred very panicky refugees. Shortly afterwards the farm came under shell fire, causing the hundred refugees to flee in all directions, leaving an old man to die in the hands of the Company Runner.

From this farm there was an excellent view of the ground leading up to the canal, and a section of MGs was sited on the top floor to give covering fire. Lt McLean then led No. 12 Platoon at the double and in open formation to the canal bank. This was carried out under heavy and sustained Spandau fire from the far bank and mortar fire from the area of Lungurella. The latter could be seen by "D" Company OP and was successfully engaged by 496 Battery of 132 Field Regiment RA. There was found a small bridge, partly blown, and scrambling across, No. 12 Platoon attacked a farm some two hundred yards on the far side of the canal. Five prisoners were taken in this farm, the sixth member having been shot by Lieut RR McLean in a pistol duel.

When No. 12 Platoon was finally established in the area of this farm they were joined by the remainder of the Company and the advance was continued on Lungurella itself.

The resistance was indeed fanatical for not one of the ten positions that were encountered up to nightfall would give in, each having to be silenced in turn.

By nightfall the opposition had so stiffened that it was found impossible to advance any further, but "B" Company was now only five hundred yards from Lungurella. They were therefore ordered to dig in and await complete dark when "A" Company would attack through them and capture the bridge South of Lungurella. During this advance "B" Company's casualties had been negligible but they had accounted for some fourteen in dead and had now taken twenty-eight prisoners.

Shortly after "B" Company had forced the crossing of the canal, Lt Col HMA Hunter, MBE, was ordered to return to "B" Echelon for rest, for he had not slept during the past three days and the strain was beginning to tell on him. The 2 i/c, Major ME Fisher, MC, then took over command of the Battalion.

Throughout the afternoon "D" Company had been lying up in the area of the farm seventy five yards to the South of the canal, and just opposite Lungurella, engaging with both small arms and artillery anything they saw moving. It was apparent that the enemy suspected this farm as containing an OP, for it was continually being stonked by both artillery and mortars.

At about 1700 hours, after "B" Company had secured their bridgehead across the canal and were advancing on Lungurella, it was decided by Major ME Fisher, MC, for a platoon attack to be made over the canal to capture a group of buildings which lay on the outskirts of Lungurella and thereby to divert the attention of the enemy from the main advance along the Northern bank of the Canal by "B" Company.

At this point the canal was about forty feet wide, and seven feet deep, and the bridge, as it was shortly learned, had been blown and so could not afford a means of crossing. No. 17 Platoon, "D" Company — commanded by Lieut JWC Ledger — went forward to make the attack supported by artillery and MG fire. They reached the bank without incident, but when Lieut Ledger and Cpl Donovan started to move over the bank to make a recce for a crossing place they were met with such withering MG fire from well dug-in positions on the opposite bank that Cpl Donovan was wounded and Lt Ledger had great difficulty in getting him back to the safety of the bank.

It was apparent that a daylight attack was not practicable, and 17 Platoon was accordingly withdrawn to the area of the farm houses.

A night attack was then planned, to be undertaken by "A" Company, in which that Company was to attack through the firm base that was being held by "B" Company on the far side of the canal and only four hundred yards from Lungurella, against repeated counter attacks.

At 2300 hours on the 21st this attack, which proved to be the final phase of the battle for, and leading up to Lungurella, was launched. The attack took place in the full light of burning hayricks and farm outhouses, and by 2345 hours Nos 7 and 8 Platoons had gained their last objective — the bridge across the canal leading to Lungurella. No Opposition had been met and only two wounded prisoners had been taken. The enemy had fled.

At 0100 hours on the 22nd, "B" Company occupied Lungurella without opposition, followed by "C" Company, "D" Company and Main HQ.

The REs immediately set about constructing a Bailey across the canal, and by 0600 hours the bridge had been completed and the Battalion "B" Echelon was roaring across.

It was then learned that other troops of the Division had reached the area of Ferrara, principal objective South of the Po, and so, the expected and hoped for rest after the past arduous 48 hours could not now be had, for within a few hours the Battalion was once again on the move chasing the now exhausted and fast disintegrating enemy forces.

Night Advance through il Quartiere
(See map VI).

2nd Battalion the Lancashire Fusiliers.

By April 18th, Argenta had been cleared and the enemy was on the run. By their crossing of the Fossa Marina, 2 L. F. had played a large part in clearing a way for the armoured striking force, and the Battalion now hoped to have a day or two's rest. Companies had concentrated on the 18th, and mobile baths were arranged for the following day, However, late in the afternoon orders were received to be ready to move at midnight. The Battalion was to move from the Argenta area, to Stazione Di Consandolo, with the proviso "If you can't get there, get as near to it as you can". 2nd Armoured Brigade and LIR were driving for the intact bridges across the Fossa Di Porto, West of Portomaggiore; If the bridges were secured, the Battalion was to reinforce the LIR, if not, the Battalion was to remain under command 11 Brigade.

An advance party was sent ahead under Major K. Hill, MC, to arrange a concentration area in the new location. The Battalion left Argenta at midnight, no longer a Battalion, but a Battalion group. Apart from TCVs, there were the BHQ vehicles, S Company, a Platoon of Kensington MMGs, a Platoon of their 4.2 mortars, and a troop of M 10. Information regarding the roads was slight, and all that was known was that an armoured formation had covered the area. It was a strange journey, with fires blazing along the route, and the sound of battle to the left rear, between Argenta and Consandolo on Route 16. Eventually the column was confronted by a blow in the road East of Consandolo: many possibilities of flanking moves were explored. Only one way round was found, and this was blocked by a 3-tonner which had collapsed through a bridge. The C.O. went see O.C. 2nd Armoured Brigade and was instructed to have the Battalion ready for action by dawn. As it was impossible to reach the original location, another area was found where it was possible to get off the road. Breakfast was immediately prepared, and consumed by dawn.

At first light it was possible to recce a new route to the original conc. area at Consandolo St. and the Battalion arrived there at 0600 hours. After a hasty night move, a battle was to be expected soon, but it did not take place. All day the Battalion remained on the alert, and the C.O. was called to 11 Brigade HQ.

to whose command the Battalion had reverted. Several tentative plans were made: at one time the Battalion was to cross the Fossa di Porto, at another it was to go through Portomaggiore. The day was perhaps the most exasperating, of many exasperating occasions. A sudden move in the night was followed by a seemingly endless period of waiting. In the late afternoon the C.O. received orders to pass through a small bridge-head formed by the LIR across the Fossa di Porto. The Battalion was then to advance westwards along the bank, turning North along the road through Il Quartiere and finally westwards again to the bridge over the Canale San Nicolo. The canal was to be crossed and the advance continued. No enemy worth mentioning were expected — possible the odd chap. Such statements had been made before, in the history of the Battalion.

The C.O. I.O. and OCs "D" and "B" Companies went down to the river to visit the LIR forward Company, to obtain a view of the country over which the Battalion was to advance at night. Meanwhile the 2 i/c had recce'd an assembly area for the Battalion at Ripapersico. The C.O.s plan was as follows: — D, B, A, C, Companies were to advance in this order with the axis as previously described. The advance was not to commence until a bridge had been completed across the Fossa di Porto, fit for all types of traffic. The estimated time for the completion of the bridge was midnight, but in fact it turned out to be somewhat later. The Battalion moved to the assembly area at dusk on the 19th, with a squadron of tanks that had joined it in the morning. Owing to the lack of time, the O Group was held in the assembly area. The only light was found in the room occupied by the REs, and they were somewhat disconcerted by the influx of people. By midnight the Battalion was ready to move, and waited only for the signal from Brigade to cross the bridge. A bridge had been made by bulldozing in the banks of the river, which is divided into two separate branches. During the bulldozing the area attracted considerable harrassing fire, and there was some anxiety lest enemy activity should impede the crossing. The Companies crossed without difficulty, but some congestion was caused by the transport. Until the bridge-head could be expanded by the leading Company, there was little room for the transport and tanks which accompanied the Battalion, and which were not likely to be needed before dawn. 1 Surreys were following immediately behind the Battalion and hence it was necessary for the Battalion to get clear of the bridge area as soon as possible.

At approx. 0100 hours OC "D" Company, Major P. Henshall, MC, went forward to liase with the LIR Company Commander on the far bank of the canal. He was informed on arrival that the enemy appeared still to be holding Il Quartiere in some strength. On the strength of this information a preliminary shoot was put down on Il Quartiere and also on the canal bank along which the Company was destined to advance before reaching the village. About 2330 hours "D" Company the leading Company reached the first objective just South of the village. During this short advance already 20 PWs had been taken, and it thus seemed as if the way was not to be so clear of enemy as the Battalion had been informed. The tanks were unable to follow the Company up to this point owing to the presence of a ditch 10 ft wide and 8 ft deep which had to be bulldozed in.

As the operation consisted of an advance guard and not an attack on a definite objective a pre-arranged barrage had not been included in the plan. The route of the advance was however covered by a series of stonks in depht available on call. Once inside Il Quartiere the leading Company found the scene extremely grim. At first sight the place appeared completely deserted, but the Platoon moving up on the side of the road soon discerned flitting shadows retiring from house to house. A heavy volley of fire broke out from all sides, but it would seem that the enemy were in no fit state to stand and fight, his sole concern was to escape as swiftly and as soundlessly as possible.

Shortly before dawn "D" Company had secured and cleared the area of the village Il Quartiere. As "B" Company passed through to continue the advance a stonk of considerable intensity unfortunately descended in the Company areas. Some 500 shells fell and a number of casualties were caused, including an Officer who was killed. "A" Company was temporarily disorganised, and remained in

Il Quartiere as reserve. Progress was maintained until the area of the road junction was reached North of the village. The Squadron of tanks in support had crossed the obstacle at dawn, and had been supporting the advance from Il Quartiere. The road junction was obviously an enemy strongpoint, and all approaches were well covered by MG fire. Whilst fire from SP guns was discouraging activity on the part of our tanks. One enemy SP, or tank nipped round the bend in the road and hit one of our leading tanks, making good its retreat before fire was returned by the tanks. Several attacks by "B" Company were repelled during the morning, and any approach to the road junction produced an intense volume of MG fire. Finally "B" Company succeeded in outflanking the road junction, and seized some buildings on the road to the West. With these buildings firmly held, it was possible to sweep down to the road junction. In this operation the BHQ of 98 Fusilier Battalion, and most of its staff was captured. Some 25 PWs were taken, including an Officer. The C.O. however, was able to escape on foot.

To secure the left flank, "C" Company had been sent out to the flank from Il Quartiere, and had reached the line of the canal. Information was received that two Battalions of 38 Brigade were passing through in the night, along the original axis of the Battalion. 5 Northamptons were advancing along the axis of the railway line. To facilitate their advance the Battalion was ordered to clear the area between the road junction North of Il Quartiere and the road and rail crossing. This task was accomplished by "D" Company, with the assistance of a barrage, arranged by 322 Battery Commander, Major R. Horne. The Battalions of 38 Brigade passed through at midnight, and the operation of the Battalion was momentarily ended.

Casualties from enemy sources were not heavy, but the stonk which fell on the forward Company inflicted a number of fatal, and non fatal casualties. 2 Officers were killed, and 2 other Officers were wounded on other occassions.

This advance by the Battalion had been particularly tricky. A number of factors had contributed to make the operation difficult. In the first place the familiar sequence of night moves followed by a day of alerted inactivity, and its consequent loss of sleep, had got on everybody's nerves. Secondly, the time for the C.O. to formulate his plans had been far too short, so that final orders for the advance had to be issued in the Assembly Area. This lack of time was also a heavy burden on the artillery, as it gave them little time to work out their plans in detail. Thirdly, the change from Battalion to Battalion Group, greatly increased the responsibility of the C.O. and his staff. The anti-tank, and the support group platoons were under command of the Battalion, and this widened the scope of any plan the C.O. had to make. Fourthly, only negligible opposition was forecast, and this did not turn out to be the case. fifthly, owing to the nature of the operation, an advance guard, as opposed to a set attack, less planning could be done before the operation commenced, and more had to be left to planning as the operation developed.

36th Infantry Brigade

(See map. V).

The Buffs at Benvignante

5th Battalion the Buffs.

The Argylls were attacking Consandolo. Their struggle had been bitter and prolonged, but by four o'clock they reached it and cleared it, but were too tired to exploit their success. So it had been decided that the Buffs should go through them and thrust beyond.

But as you stand around waiting you don't know this. All you are aware of is that ghastly uncertainty and the fact that you are tired of doing nothing.

But there is movement at last. Companies are filing away and soon yours is doing the same, section by section, slowly and mostly silent. It is growing dusk now. The sun has gone and the light is dying. Just enough for you to see your comrade's face. You wonder whether you are looking as strained and tense as he.

A few miles at the most and then a halt. Great ungainly shapes dot the grey fields. Tanks. The air seems somehow lighter. Tanks are with you to-night. You will have their support. Somebody says that tanks bring down enemy fire, that the noise they create gives your positions away, but the general opinion is favourable towards them.

Another period of waiting. You stretch out beside the great silent shapes and smoke the last cigarette. You doze or talk in whispers. The story has been circulated that you are to pass through the Jocks and push on for as far as you can go. You snatch at every whisper of a rumour as though it were Holy Writ. You drag on your cigarette and watch the moon enter the sky.

Movement. Men getting to their feet, tank-crews clambering into their vehicles. At last. You adjust your equipment and try to distribute weight evenly. At last. Waiting is over and you are on the move.

The first company is away accompanied by its clattering escort. The melee sorts itself out; a delay is caused by the leading company taking the wrong road, but at last you are really away, crossing a field and so on to a good road. The road to Consandolo, where the Argylls wait, and beyond that — who knows? But at least you are moving and that is something.

You feel happier as you march. The clatter and iron clangour of the tanks is comforting to you. You talk or sing softly to yourself. There is no need for silence with those monsters bellowing all around.

Consandolo. Ruined town. Roads littered with debris. Houses shapeless hulks or untidy heaps. Shadowy figures standing with rifle or tommy-gun. The glint of an eye beneath the dark shadow of a steel helmet. A whispered word.

"Are you the Buffs?"

"Yes. What's on Jock?"

"Nothing much now. Quiet enough."

"Think he's pulled out?"

"Couldn't say. May have. Goodnight chum."

"Goodnight Jock."

And that was Consandolo. The Argylls are in it after a long and sticky day's work. And you are through it while beyond lies anything. And the night is young.

As you march you are watching to your left, the man in front to the right, watching for a movement or moonshine on metal, watching for a red spurt that may mean death. It is so silent. Not a sound except those of your own making.

Time passes. You trudge a few hundred yards and stop. Why you stop you don't know. There is just a muttered command, and the long snake of burdened men halts. You have covered quite some distance now and weight is making itself felt. Bren guns are passed from shoulder to shoulder; the P.I.A.T. is an abomination. Ammunition weighs heavy, but the darkness, half lit by the moon, seems to weigh heaviest of all. Now you see men squatting by the roadside when the slow but steady advance is checked. Now you see them stretched on the dusty highway, snatching each precious moment of relaxation. Only a few stand erect, braced against the burden they carry, casting shapeless inky shadows on the white road.

How quiet it is. The tanks seem to have gone ahead. You hear their metallic clatter in the distance, but apart from that it is deadly quiet. Only the croaking of frogs from roadside ditches, the muted mutter of a word or two and the steady scuffling crunch of trudging feet.

It is a lovely night. How often have you seen a night quite so beautiful? English nights in April at their best, soft and mild as the fairest lawn fresh and unsoiled, with the clean sweet smell of hedgerow and garden, field and coppice and a hand in yours. An English lane and the dews falling soft and rare about you, and footsteps at your side. The scuffling crunch of heavy boots on flinty road surface, the muttered exclamations blend into an insignificant background. Like a squirrel in its cage your thoughts revolve, — past and present, past present, cycle complete, — pent up by the light starry sky overhead, that ragged black hedgerow on one side and open grey misted field on the other, and the hard gritted road beneath your feet.

Instinctive change of shoulder for your weapon, a brace to your shoulders and a deeper breath of cool air. How much longer? How far? How long till the dawn? and after that . . . . . Suddenly the peace and quiet is evil. You feel that something is going to happen soon and suddenly and unless you are wary you will not survive it. You strive even harder to pierce the gloom all about you and wish the moon were high again.

Another halt. The blurred figures melt into the road surface. A whisper runs down the file. A movement and it is galvanised into life. It surges and sways and blurs across the white road into hedge and ditch. The grass is wet and the fragrance of bruised mint is heavy in the air. You are alert now. You lie flat and whisper one to another.

"They've bumped him. A house. Two houses. A village. The tanks are going forward. Keep your eyes open now, for Christ's sake." You lie in the ditch and watch the road. But what of the field behind you? That may be nursing death secretly and silently. Suddenly with the abruptness of a heart bursting, there is a flash and a crash and an acrid stench. You shiver and cower, then brace yourself to stare again. Voices, shouting, strangely loud and highly nervous. Again the whisper runs fleet foot from lip to lip.

"A bazooka. For God's sake watch out."

Your eyes are aching and swimming with strain. Voices again. A flash and a crash that makes you wince. Another. Another. Whisper .....

"Tanks. Shelling the house."

Fascinated you watch as round after round crash into the doomed building. A pause and then the sharp high crackle of Besa fire. Tracers curve and dance across the sky ricochetting like phosphorus hornets. A pause — and again the crash of cannon fire. The house is burning, madly, a gorgeous scarlet flower growing every minute. Outhouses, stacks, barns are added to the beauty of it.

Figures on the road. A huddled group and one walking behind with a pointed rifle. Prisoners. They tramp past and you raise yourself in the damp grass to see others approaching. What is happening forward? The worst of war is that you never see a complete picture. Follow the road past the pool of ruddy light from the burning house, past the silent grim watchful tank, past the little group beside it, farther into the unknown and so to the leading Company. A moment of confusion and then the road was clear again, but from the hedge and ditch came the sharp short rapping of Bren and the crack of rifles. Confusion in the air. Figures that flitted from bush to bush, German voices and white rags fluttering, then onwards again. The village Benvignante. The first faint light of dawn and the smoke of burning houses heavy and pungent. Men blinking into each others faces, standing in little knots at doorways, resting equipment, others stretched behind Brens at vantage points. A checking and counter-checking and a feeling of success. The longest night march of the campaign is at its end and the infantry had outstripped the armour and were through the gap at last. The enemy were making helter-skelter for the Po crossings, and final Victory was brought a step nearer. But success is a bubble so easily broken......

Passing through the main cluster of buildings which comprise Benvignante, a Company has pressed forward to secure a screen about it, to consolidate and make assurance doubly sure that the enemy had actually left.

Isolated patches of resistance crackle like twigs beneath their feet. A mortar team is captured without much trouble, and the feeling of success and confidence mounts higher. The fascination of the hunt grips everybody. Fatigue is forgotten.

A cluster of houses is the next objective. The dawn is clear and grey now with the tang of burning heavy in it.

The first house yields only signs of occupation and hurried flight. The second snaps back with a fusillade of shots from Spandau and Schmeisser. But it is only a gesture. Soon that too is disgorging solemn prisoners and presently an O.P. is established in it. It seems all over now. Success is complete and whole, like a covetted trophy in the hands.

And then as the daylight strengthens and the morning mists are shot with the rising sun, comes change and the bitter taste of frustration.

The ugly ominous shapes of enemy S.P. guns break cover. The sentry can hardly trust his eyes. His shout brings confusion but it is almost drowned as with a belch of flame and smoke the leading S.P. speaks. Enemy infantry dash from yet another house and run to where another dimly seen monster lurks. Again the crash and scream of a shell. A tank which has escorted the infantry during their long march recoils and shudders, and all about it hangs a pall of heavy greasy smoke and the cries of voices. Again and again. Men are demoralised.

Orders are being shouted. Reliability springs from all ranks at this crisis as they react according to the stuff of which the are made. A Serjeant seizes a P.I.A.T. and standing boldly fires it at an S.P. gun in a magnificent gesture that does much to restore courage and morale. The O.P. is hit and wreathed in dust and smoke. The noise of firing gun and screaming shell is deafening at such point blank range, but somehow the men are reformed and fall back to the first house. The S.P's creep menacingly forward. It is deadly fascinating to see them; to see them creep and shudder as they give tongue; to feel the hot breath of the blast as the muzzle points straight for you, it seems; to see the flying debris at the impact and to know that death is with you, touching your elbow.

But they have steadied. A few have lost their nerve and retreated, but the rest hold while air is crackling with calls for assistance. And the enemy guns do not press home, but content themselves with flogging the houses, flinging shells down the road and across the fields into Benvignante.......

Where you are at action stations. In upper rooms Bren guns posted with supplies of magazines and loaders. You fire until your barrel is smoking hot and pray that there will be none of the stoppages the text books speak of. It fires when by rights it should be seized up. It fires, and fires again, and the spent cartridges fly about your ringing ears.

A house with a red roof set at an oblique angle from you has strange occupants. You knock a hole through your wall so as to cover it and wait. Some one with glasses stands alert. He sees a Hun poke a Spandau cautiously round the corner. It crackles electrically down the length of the street. Your comrade says "Now!" And you fire a burst. With a crash and a scream a shell scores a direct hit upon a house sheltering a platoon just across the road to you. Through the dust and smoke figures dash across the swept higway into fresh shelter. Still you fire your gun. Another magazine and another. Shells are landing all about, rear, front, flanks, but somehow your house is not touched. It quivers and shakes and every moment you except to see the wall leap at you, but it stands. There are keen eyed spotters after the enemy guns. The radio crackles directions. Another shell very close, there is a shout that somebody is hit A name you know is spoken. But you don't leave your position. Instead you concentrate a bit harder and hug the Bren as though it were your one hope of salvation, the spent cartridge cases flying like thrashed corn, the loaders scrabbing and rattling on the floor filling magazines. Another long burst at the house where the Spandau plays hide and seek. Did you get him? nobody is sure. Your gun barrel radiates in hot quivering waves of air. Your thoughts fly up the road and you wonder what is happening there.

There they are tensely waiting for the infantry to follow up behind the prowling S.P. guns, but although there are spasmodic attempts, bursts of firing diligently answered, a large scale attack is not launched. In the débris some body is groaning... but they can do nothing.

The minutes creep by. Every man's whole faculties are concentrated in ears and eyes. They are calmer, watchful and silent. Each man has his thoughts, but outwardly they are composed.

The minutes tick on. Now there is a rustle of whisper, the usual flurry of rumour passed from mouth to mouth. What is happening? Is this the real thing or just a delaying movement? Where are our tanks, our artillery? Is another Company coming up to reinforce us? The whole affair has not lasted an hour, but it seems an age since the S.P. first stirred and spoke from concealment.

Another shell. Dropping short? Another. What is this?

They are our shells, pounding houses to rubble, ploughing fields and sowing death in the fertile soil. Tight lipped they crouch and watch. A burst of flame like an orange-blossoming flower as one of the half-hidden S.P. guns heaves up and cracks open like a nut beneath a hammer. The barrage beats its patch onwards like a giant beater after game. The bright sunlight is eclipsed and through the drifting clouds they catch glimpses of burning houses and erupting fields.

A movement behind them as they watch and figures are creeping stealthily through. The artillery stops and they press forward, past the blazing S.P. gun, past the crumpled tank, past the houses recently quitted.....

In Benvignante, where the shelling has almost ceased, a patrol is going out to the house at which you had been firing. You watch them slip across the highway, vanish into the fields and trees. Out of sight for a few moments then briefly seen as one by one they dart across open ground to the rear of the house. You wait...... A stretcher party moves along the road, flag fluttering.

The patrol re-appears and eventually rejoins the main party.

Report..... Nothing there. Plenty of signs but nobody there now. You know that they are probing again forward and you wait expectantly, but nothing happens and gradually you allow yourself to think that the counter-attack has been beaten off.

You relax and light a cigarette.

The stretcher party returning reports that all seems well now. You have held your gains of that previous night. Those precious eight miles are still intact.

And you tired. Conscious of being hungry but curiously elated later you stand at the door and watch the pursuit sweep on.

In a matter of hours what was the very tip of the advance becomes the rear. A continuous stream of armour crashes by, lorried infantry, Buffaloes, bridge building stores. You look at your comrades and laugh and say "We're Base Wallahs now!"

But for all things a price has to be paid. It was paid this time as always. Men you knew are no more, men who set out on that night march marched into a deeper night with the dawn.

Honour their memory as the pursuit rolls onwards; honour their memory a little later as the curtain goes down on the Italian Campaign; as the tracers fly skywards; as the mortar flares drift in pools of blinding light, startling the night; as the verey flares, green and red, pale the stars; and that complete Victory which grinned at you like a death's head on Monte Grande becomes reality at last.

The Argylls on the Road to Ferrara
(See map VI).

By a platoon Commander of the 8th Argyll and Sutherland Highlanders.

After a few days rest in Consandolo the Battalion moved off again. This time the axis of advance was Route 16 and the final objective was an important cross-roads dominating the main route to Ferrara. The general plan was for the battalion to push on as fast as possible and whenever the leading company met opposition it was to deal with it and the next company would bypass and take the lead. We had close support from Churchill Tanks. The Battalion started off at 1730 hours on the 21st April led by R Company, with X, B, and Y following in that order. During the remaining hours of daylight all companies came under heavy and accurate fire from Boche S.P. guns. A shell landed a few yards from one of my corporals who was carrying that unpopular burden a PIAT on his shoulder. The blast blew the corporal over and caused him to part company with his PIAT but he quickly picked himself up and merely vociferated his deeply felt objections to being sniped at with high velocity guns. Just before dark R Company and then X Company took intermediate objectives they had been given, and my company (B) passed through to attack a small village of rather scattered houses and farms. About half a mile short of the village was a large house which was to be tackled first. As 12 Platoon led off across the start line they came under heavy shell fire and had a large number of casualties. Despite this setback they carried on and soon captured the house. At this point Major Chris Burn the Company Commander ordered me to take my platoon (11) through and make for the village. Darkness had now fallen and we felt more comfortable as the shelling from the enemy had ceased owing to lack of observation. A strong fighting patrol from 11 Platoon moved into the village now and three prisoners were quickly taken from well entrenched and cleverly concealed positions just on the outskirts of the village. Information from these prisoners was to the effect that the enemy force holding the village had withdrawn during the afternoon leaving only a small rearguard to hold up our advance. This rearguard however had other ideas and were only too pleased to come out with their hands up and speak their only words of English "I surrender". These Boche disposed of, the Patrol Commander reported the village clear of enemy and the rest of B Company moved in to consolidate and wait for Y Company to pass through. At this stage my platoon H.Q. was established in a large cattle shed which stank as only an Italian cattle shed can. The men not on sentry were relaxing, sitting about talking about the days work and things in general. They were in very good form. My signaller told me that he had come across a civilian in the shed and that though he had spoken to him in his best Italian he couldnt make the civilian understand. This didnt surprise me as he spoke with the broadest of Scots accents. However we investigated and discovered that the so-called civilian was a German soldier trying to make good his escape. We obtained some valuable information from him.

We now heard from Battalion H.Q. that Y Company had taken the next objective and X Company followed by us were to move on again to the cross-roads which had been given as our final task. This proved very easy and X Company were soon consolidating round the cross-roads. This meant that we were sitting astride the main Ferrara lateral road. It was apparent that the Germans had no idea we were so far on. A Volkswagen with three ocupants soon came down the road from Ferrara and was held up by Lt. "Winnie" Wainwright, our Pioneer Officer, who had insisted on transferring to the leading company each time a change in order of march was made. Unfortunately for "Winnie" while he was still holding up and interrogating the prisoners, some of his men searched the car and removed all the loot. So well had the advance gone that the Battalion Commander ordered B Company to move on again through X Company along the road in the direction of Ferrara. This had to be done cautiously as we had no information about the enemy and they certainly didnt know we were about. Deep ditches on either side of the road provided excellent cover for the advancing troops and we made good time for about half an hour without opposition. Then for the second time transport was heard coming from the direction of Ferrara. This time there was definitely more than one vehicle, and quick orders were given to 11 Platoon to prepare an ambush. All platoon weapons were quickly in position, including the Piat which the corporal had had blown off his shoulder earlier. When the leading vehicle of the three had only a few yards away, the signal was given and every man in the platoon opened up. The vehicles skidded to a standstill with a screeching of brakes and in a few seconds it was all over. Only one driver was still alive, and although he was badly wounded he was only too keen to answer any questions put to him.

Just then we were told to stop our advance and dig in — the final phase in every infantry battle. The men were tired but their morale was at its highest. We had had a long night advance with a fair amount of opposition, there had been casualties and very trying enemy shelling. But we had taken all objectives, seen prisoners come in and above all we were going forward fast. Everyone knew that the end was approaching at last. There would be no stopping us now.

38 (Irish) Infantry Brigade

(See map IV).

The last Offensive — The Santerno Brigdehead

By the Commander of 38 Irish Infantry Brigade.

On the morning of the 10th I held a final conference at Brigade Headquarters in Forli to go through the plan that appeared to be the most likely one for us to embark on. The grouping was designed to be appropriate to any variety of the plan that might be dictated by future events. The Brigade Group that we handled during the Santerno bridgehead phase was about the size of an Armoured Division. In addition to our own battalions, our armour included the 2nd Armoured Brigade (less the 10th Hussars), 4th Hussars, B Squadron 51 Royal Tank Regiment (Flails), C Squadron 51 Royal Tank Regiment (Crocodiles), an armoured assault troop R. E., a dozer troop R. E. The artillery under command was the 17th Field Regiment, 11 R. H. A., Z troop 209 Self Propelled Battery, 254 Anti-Tank Battery, and the support of as much of the remainder of the Divisional artillery as we could use, which included a medium regiment. In addition of course we had our 214 Field Company R. E., 152 Field Ambulance, and D Support Group.

The object of our operation was to pass through the 8 Indian Division's bridgehead over the Santerno, about Mondaniga, swing North between the West bank of the Santerno and the Scolo Fossatone, and capture the bridge over the River Reno near Bastia, an advance of about 12,000 yards. Obviously this was too deep an attack to carry through with the same units leading as there was no reason to suppose that the Germans would not contest every yard of the way from their well prepared positions. I therefore had three elements to undertake this task — a breaking out force, a mobile force to follow through, and the reserve force for special roles. This mobile force was entirely mounted on tracked vehicles, and should be able to maintain a uniform speed of cross country performance throughout all its units and sub-units. The object of The mobile force, under command of Brigadier John Coombe, was to be ready to pass through the breaking out force as soon as that force had either shot its bolt, or the going appeared to be favourable for the armour. I hoped to be able to pass this force through as soon as the breaking out force had cleared up to the bottle neck at La Giovecca. We hoped that the speed of the final advance might bounce the River Reno bridge which was our objective.

In detail, the grouping was as follows: —

THE BREAK OUT FORCE.

1 R. Ir. F.	2 INNISKS
A Squadron BAYS	B Squadron BAYS
D Support Group MMG Platoon	C Squadron 51 R. T. R. (Crocodiles)
Reconnaissance Party R. E.	D Support Group MMG Platoon
Scissors Bridge	Reconnaissance Party R. E.
Bulldozer Troop R. E.	

ARTILLERY IN IMMEDIATE SUPPORT.

17 Field Regiment R. A.   11 R. H. A.

THE MOBILE FORCE (KANGAROO ARMY)

Headquarters 2 Armoured Brigade   Z Troop 209 S. P. Battery
9 LANCERS   Assault Detachment R. E.
4 HUSSARS (Kangaroos)   2 L. I. R.

RESERVES FOR SPECIAL ROLES.

C Squadron BAYS   D Support Group Mortar Platoon
254 Anti-Tank Battery   214 Field Company R. E.
S. P. Troop 254 Anti-Tank Battery   152 Field Ambulance.
Armoured Troop R. E.

At 1300 hours on the 10th we left Forli and concentrated, less the armour, South of Bagnacavallo. Our teeing up was really being done in stages. We had two assembly areas East of the Senio — one for infantry and one for armour, and we had a marrying up area near Lugo on the West of the Senio. It was necessary to assemble fairly near the Senio in order that we might start making use of the bridges as soon as they were ready. If possible infantry and tanks should never cross an obstacle in the same place, and so there was no object in bringing them together until they had got across the river by their different routes. We got into our assembly area without incident, and in the light of the latest information I issued verbal orders for the move to the wedding area West of the Senio where the tanks and infantry would join up, to start at 6 o'clock the next morning.

This move went without incident, and slowly but surely we gathered up all the bits and pieces that were to form our force. At 9 o'clock that evening I held a co-ordinating conference in Lugo, checked over the plan and the tying up of all the Group, and made provisional arrangements for the order of march forward. During this night the 8 Indian Division were to form their bridgehead over the Santerno and to link up with the New Zealand Division, who had already got troops across in some places, but whose bridgehead was not yet formed.

One of the characteristics of crossing rivers is the conflicting and often contradictory information that one receives over the state of bridges. One person says a bridge will be ready in two hours, then it is put back to six, then someone else says it was ready half an hour ago. The next thing that happens is that something falls in. We had learned that the only way to overcome this is by direct communication to our own representative at the bridge site. Even that does not overcome the human factor of incorrect estimates of time required to complete a job. The main point was that we were in a good position to get across the Santerno bridge as soon as it was ready. Apart from a few harmless shells that were scattered around Lugo we suffered no discomforts.

About half past eleven on the 12th the Santerno bridgehead was beginning to look pretty good, and bridges were expected to be ready some-time during the afternoon. The general advance on our Northern flank was such that a variation to the original Divisional plan could be made. In the original plan 36 Brigade were to sweep North along the east of the Santerno while we were on the West. It seemed unlikely that organized resistance East of the river would amount to anything very much, and the wise alternative of switching 36 Brigade on to our left and merely using some of the Reconnaissance Regiment on the East of the river was decided upon. 36 Brigade were to strike out in a Westerly direction towards San Patrizio and Conselice, and so give us more elbow room to jump off and cover our flank. To be of most value in this role it was clearly necessary that 36 Brigade should move first, and fortunately the lay-out in the wedding area permitted this to be done without any difficulty.

They started off about 4 o clock and were able to begin their attack that evening. We had also hoped to start that evening, but congestion on the tracks and bridges and the shelling of our bridge delayed matters so much that we could not manage it. The attack was therefore postponed until dawn, and the Faughs were told to maintain contact that night by patrolling. The Indians kept contact on the Skin's front.

0630 hours on the 13th was the Zero hour for our breaking out force.

36 Brigade in the meanwhile had done well and gave us considerable elbow room on our left flank. The Germans must have been a bit foxed when we turned North that morning, as 36 Brigade's advance would have made them expect the main thrust to be in a Westerly direction.

I left Main Brigade in the wedding area and established a Tactical HQ just East of Mondaniga with John Coombe, Margot Asquith commanding the Bays, Rupert Lecky commanding the 17th Field Regiment, and with John McClinton as assistant.

I was very keen for the Faughs to get some elements of infantry and tanks across the Scolo Fossatone to cover the left flank. This was more easily said than done, but fortunately with the assistance of the Assault R.Es we got them across. As the advance went Northwards to the bottle-neck at La Giovecca, the frontage between the Santerno and the Fossatone narrowed down to less than a thousand yards. I felt it was important that we should be on a rather broader front than this if we were to have room to get the ponderous Kangaroo Army through the Gap.

The nature of the country was true to the form that I have previously described. Although not yet in leaf the vines and trees restricted visibility to about 100 yards and provided excellent cover for small determined parties on both sides. Especially did it help the Bosche bazooka men. Eenemy strongpoints were continually being met, but by the speedy and determined efforts of the tank-cum-infantry packets they were soon dealt with.

The strongest resistance was probably met about the line running East and West through San Bernardino. Elements of the 8th Indian Division were advancing on this place from the East but even so the Skins had a tough time in this sector. The Bosche were sitting tight in their holes and it took quite a lot of determined work to kill or capture them.

By about midday both battalions were approaching the La Giovecca bottle-neck, and the moment seemed ripe to unleash John Coombe and his Kangaroo Army.

It was a difficult job getting so many armoured vehicles through this thick country and to pass them through our foremost troops. I had arranged for recognition signals to be fired by verey pistol to indicate our forward positions to the approaching tanks, but even with this aid they found great difficulty in determining friend from foe. Leading elements of the mobile force were beginning to take on the enemy by about 1330. I include here the London Irish account of this phase of the battle: —

"The object of the Kangaroo Army was to secure crossings over the Conselice Canal and if possible exploit to the River Reno, several thousands of yards ahead.

At first little resistance was encountered. The Skins and the Faughs had given the enemy a good shaking and he was on the move back. Scattered enemy Bazooka men were met and one tank was lost through the fire of an anti-tank gun, but a number of prisoners were taken by G Company.

As the Conselice Canal was approached the rivers opened out, and H Company with C Squadron of the 9th Lancers came up on the left. Resistance was encountered in the village of La Frascata. This was immediately bypassed, but as the leading tanks arrived at the canal the bridge was blown up immediately in front of them. H Company, who had driven past La Frascata in their Kangaroos, speedily de-bussed on the banks of the canal and, covered by the tanks, forced a crossing over the remains of the road and railway bridges, getting into the houses on the far bank so rapidly that few of the defenders managed to escape.

Meanwhile G Company was clearing the area up to the canal bank on the right and E Company was ordered to clear La Frascata and assist H Company in holding and enlarging the bridgehead. The enemy had been surprised by the speed and weight of the attack. Few of them, not more than ten, had been killed, but all three forward companies had taken numbers of prisoners. By 1830 hours the total was eighty.

The bridgehead was firmly established by 2200 hours and Companies were dug in for the night. Sappers were building a bridge over the canal, the armour was in leaguer and plans for the following day were being made. A large increase in the number of wrist watches possessed by H Company was noticed.

Early on the 14th, before dawn, patrols from E Company were feeling their way up through Lavezzola towards the R. Reno. At first light they were followed by the armour in two columns, one due North along the axis of the main road and the other sweeping round to the right to avoid the mine-fields that were known to exist in the Lavezzola area. The whole area was heavily mined and the houses booby trapped in the northern half of the village, but luckily the German mine warning notices were still in place and not a single casualty was caused to either tanks or Infantry. The flails had a great morning exploding mines.

The Reno was reached at 0940 hours, about 30 prisoners having been taken. These included eight taken in the act of laying further mines. Both the road and rail bridges over the river were gone but sufficient rubble still remained to allow foot soldiers to cross dryshod. Reconnaissance was carried out and a plan evolved for two platoons of E Company to cross and form a small bridgehead. This took place at 1230 hours without resistance and under cover of smoke, but while the platoons were advancing North from the river they were heavily counter-attacked and most of them over-run. No assistance could be given by the tanks owing to the high floodbanks and the absence of a bridge. Positions were now taken up on the near bank and further reconnaissance carried out with a view to making a deliberate crossing.

At this time 56 Division, who had landed on the southern shores of Lake Comacchio, were still several thousand yards East of this attempted bridgehead and the enemy was therefore very sensitive to a threat from their southern flank. It was however decided to hold positions on the southern bank of the river for the night and eventually the battalion was ordered to maintain these static positions for the next two days. A point of special interest which arose at this time was that the 1st Battalion London Irish on the left flank of 56 Division was, for the first time in this war, sharing a common piece of the front with this battalion, and on the first night one of their patrols crossed the Reno and contacted G Company."

On the evening of the 13th the Skins clamped down about La Giovecca and the Faughs were spread out on the West of the Fossatone watching the flank. Both battalions had fought magnificently during the day and had had a long and anxious period moving up for the battle. We captured two officers and one hundred and fifty-seven O. Rs mainly from 362 Division during the day's work.

On the 14th the London Irish were the main participants as already described by them. The Skins had a day off and the Faughs were patrolling out to the West. Brigade Headquarters were established at La Palazzina about half way between the Skins and the London Irish.

Partisans appeared in this area. They proved a mixed blessing. There were two types, those who put on their arm bands and slung their muskets round their shoulders after the Bosche had pulled out, and those who did fight genuinely, many of whom still had fresh wounds. The second variety were extremely helpful and had detailed maps and drawings showing enemy positions and minefields which later proved to be very accurate. They all, however, had one big failing, common throughout Italy. Once having allowed them to start talking nothing would induce them to stop. They held non-stop meetings throughout the day, which were soon referred to as "Partisan 'O' Groups". These meetings resembled mobile arsenals, for all the men and also the women carried at least four weapons and were festooned with bandoliers, grenades, knives and every sort of "what have you". Bala Bredin CO of 2 LIR enlisted a platoon of these scoundrels from which he was expecting great things, but I never heard much more about them. As well as the partisans, some odd members of the Cremona Gruppo got mixed up in the proceedings — I suppose they had friends in those parts.

On the 15th the Faughs sent patrols to clear up the marsh lands up to the Sillaro river. The enemy was holding the far bank in some places and had strong points in houses. That evening this clearing up job was taken over by 36 Brigade and the Faughs concentrated.

56 Division in the meanwhile had come up level with us on the North of the Reno and had passed across our front towards Bastia and Argenta so we were able to start bridging operations across the River Reno. It was estimated that the bridge would be ready for our further advance by midday the following day, and we were accordingly placed at four hours notice to continue the advance the next morning. Not only had our part of the battle gone according to plan — which is a very rare thing to happen — but the whole of the Army Group was moving according to schedule too. Everything was looking very promising, but the big battle of the Argenta Gap, on which the whole success of the 5 Corps advance depended, still lay before us. Some regrouping took place at this stage and we lost a good deal of our force. The Bays were to join 11 Brigade, and the 9th Lancers were to be with us. The 2nd Armoured Brigade from now on remained directly under Division. The Crocodiles, Flails, and Assault R. Es also left us as all those sort of things would be playing a big part in the dense minefields of the Argenta Gap.

Outflanking Argenta
(See map. V).

The 2nd Battalion The Royal Inniskilling Fusiliers.

On 16 April 1945, 2 Innisks were concentrated in La Giovecca. A Brigade 'O' Group was held at 1430 hours and plans for the breakthrough at Argenta were made. The plan was for 38 (Irish) Brigade to pass through the Lancashire Fusiliers as soon as they had secured their bridgehead over the Fossa Marina Canal. This obstacle was the largest canal that ran from Argenta in a North Easterly direction across our front. The R. Ir. F. were to go first and advance in a N. N. W. direction; 2 Innisks were to follow them and swing West. Zero hour was to be first light on 17 April. Each Battalion had its Squadron of Tanks (Queen's Bays) and normal supporting arms. The whole move was designed to outflank the town of Argenta on the East, and then cut Route 16 North of it. The plan, if successful, would seal off the town and open a way through the gap.

The C. O. issued his orders. The Battalion would advance on a two-company front, 'C' and 'D' Companies forward, 'A' Company following 'C' and 'B' Company following 'D'. Each Company had its own troop of tanks and the leading Companies each had an Artillery F.O.O.

Due to difficulty experienced by the L. Fs in crossing the Fossa Marina our advance was postponed until 1200 hours, at which time a firm bridgehead across the obstacle had been formed. Our 7 hours in the assembly area had been enlivened by a grandstand view of the MAAF bombing of the town of Argenta, only 1000 yards away to our left front.

Punctually at 1200 hours 'C' and 'D' Companies moved forward.

'D' Company's first objective was a group of houses on the right flank which were being held by the enemy as strong-points. These houses were taken by 17 Platoon without loss to themselves in spite of considerable MG fire and sniping from the left. Immediately after this a very heavy mortar 'stonk' was put down by the enemy, which completely pinned the remainder of the Company to the ground. 'D' Company's own description of this is given below: —

"The Platoon Commander led one section into a ditch, the section crowded and the Section Leader, sensing an approach of a slight panic, climbed out of the ditch with his Caubeen at a rakish angle, lit a cigarette, glared down at his men and, with supreme contempt in his voice, said 'You Bloody fools, for Jesus sake learn to behave.' The shells did not seem to worry him at all, nor his men after that."

In the advance to Route 16 North of San Antonio a total bag of two Officers and 18 OR were taken prisoner. In some farm buildings just short of Route 16 the enemy had his main force, together with a Tiger Tank. Our guns gave excellent close support, but, in spite of scoring several direct hits on the buildings, the 'Tiger' continued to pump round after round into the Company position. To return to 'D' Company's account: —

"The two leading Sections were making great progress and had managed to get within about 100 yards of the house without being spotted. When they were spotted, the enemy fired everything he had at them and the right hand section was completely pinned down, and any movement immediately attracted fire. A shell landed right amongst the left hand section wounding every one of them. A smoke screen was put down and the platoon was withdrawn having suffered 1 killed and 13 wounded."

From the left rear, the houses in Argenta continued to give trouble, and the Company Commander decided to consolidate and sent out a patrol to contact 5 Northamptons. The Company consolidated in the area of the railway line. The patrol found the Northamptons in Argenta but without Tanks, and they reported enemy Tanks in the town.

'C' Company, meanwhile, had continued their advance without very much incident. At 1445 hours however, 'A' Company, who were following 'C', were subjected to a very heavy concentration of shells from A/Tk and S.P. Guns, 'A' Company's account of this states: —

"Our leading Tank was knocked-out and 5 minutes later No. 2 Tank was set ablaze by A/Tk Gun fire. Things were looking very bad indeed, but it never put us off the job we had to do, in simple words it made us want to get at grips with the Bosche himself. 7 Platoon was moved up the road leading to the level crossing. A 'Tiger' Tank commenced firing A.P. Shells at the Platoon causing 23 casualties."

'C' Company were ordered to attack these Guns from the North West. They were eventually dealt with, and the advance continued. 'C' Company Commander reported that Route 16 was under observation by his leading troops but they could not get on to the floodbank immediately West of the road because of heavy enemy small arms fire. They had met considerable resistance from Tanks and S.P. guns, and the close of the day's fighting found two enemy tanks destroyed and two 15 cm S.P. guns abandoned

Patrols from both 'C' and 'D' Companies during the night discovered the enemy were holding the floodbank in great strength, but it was considered by both Company Commanders that a full scale attack under a barrage would carry the objective.

All night long a vigilant watch was kept by All Ranks: the enemy occupied the houses in Argenta to our left rear as well as being in strength to our immediate front.

At 0600 hours on 18 April 'D' Company again continued their attack. This time the objective was to cut Route 16. 16 Platoon was to clear the village of San Antonio, 18 Platoon the farm buildings which had given so much trouble the previous day. 17 Platoon was in reserve. To return to 'D' Company's account: —

"The Tanks made straight for the farm firing everything they had with 18 Platoon followed by 16 Platoon finding it hard to keep up. Nothing happened for the first 200 yards then the Bosche opened up with Spandau fire. Our Tanks kept up their Fire and kept him pretty well subdued. When 18 Platoon got within 100 yards of the Farm, as one man the whole Platoon swept into the house taking 12 prisoners. Here 16 Platoon swung left straight for San Antonio. They moved into this village with such speed that the enemy were taken completely by surprise, and never had a chance to make any sort of stand. They ran out of the houses and made for the Reno Floodbank. The Company Commander forestalled them in this by sending 18 Platoon straight on and swinging them left across the road to cut them off."

'D' Company had taken three other houses in rapid succession; 66 prisoners, killed 11 of the enemy and knocked-out 1 'Tiger' Tank. Amongst the prisoners was the Commander of the enemy Battalion responsible for the defence of the area and two other Officers. The Company was now firmly astablished at a large white house, situated on Route 16 near the Reno floodbank. What was more important, Argenta was now definitely cut off.

In the early afternoon the C.O. decided to attack the floodbank and capture a house 400 yards forward of 'D' Company's F.D.Ls. This attack was to be done by 'B' Company.

At 1700 hours, 'B' Company, supported by flamethrowers, attacked the floodbank West of Route 16. The Company carried its objective, and it was then discovered that the bank was not the actual Reno floodbank, but another artificial bank running parallel with Route 16, whilst the Reno floodbank swung West with the Line of the River and was actually 300 yards West of this bank. The house which was the Company's final objective was attacked under cover of the smoke from the flamethrowers and taken at the cost to the enemy of 16 wounded. The flamethrowers were withdrawn and 12 Platoon were left to mop up the area. When the smoke cleared, it became obvious that the enemy were on the Reno floodbank in great strength, and 12 Platoon found themselves being heavily attacked by 300 enemy and a 'Tiger' Tank. It later transpired that this force had formed up for a counter-attack on Argenta. Overwhelming superiority in numbers plus the difficulty in obtaining adequate artillery support close behind the floodbank, forced this Platoon to withdraw to the bank nearest the road where they were in a far better position to hit back at the enemy coming across the open ground between the two banks. 11 Platoon hastily went to their assistance, only to find themselves heavily engaged from their right by an enemy Company and two Tanks. 10 Platoon was sent to join 12 Platoon on the bank which was to be held at all costs. The Battle by this time had become hectic, and as 12 Platoon reached the bank safely a heavy artillery concentration was put down on the enemy force advancing across the open ground, inflicting many casualties. 'B' Company had now so many targets to engage that ammunition very soon ran short. 11 Platoon had inflicted so many casualties on their particular enemy force that the Tanks hoisted a Red Cross flag, picked up their casualties, and the force withdrew. This left 10 and 12 Platoons resorting to firing off Verey lights and 2" Mortar Smoke at the enemy trapped in the artillery barrage falling in front of them. Carriers with ammunition were rushed up and by 2000 hours the enemy had withdrawn.

Meanwhile, an attack by the Commando Brigade from the South West was being planned. Their attack was preceded by a heavy artillery barrage. At 2130 hours this barrage commenced. Two troops were firing out of line and their rounds fell on 'D' Company. Repeated requests to the artillery to correct this met with the answer that there were far too many guns engaged to locate the offenders and the programme must continue. 'D' Company had to "grin and bear it". Fortunately the casualties were slight. The great thing was, however that the Commando attack was successful. At 2300 hours an L.O. from this Brigade reported to Battalion Headquarters that the West bank of the Reno was clear of enemy. The Argenta Gap was now fully opened and the armour could pass through.

The Battle of the Argenta Gap proved to be the turning point of the whole campaign. If the Inniskillings had failed to achieve all they did it might have altered the whole course of the big operation of destroying the German Army South of the Po.

The Destruction of the Enemy South of the R. Po

(See map. VII).

An account by the 1st Battalion the Royal Irish Fusiliers.

At five o'clock on the 23rd April the Battalion commenced moving forward to an assembly area just South of the Bailey Bridge being constructed over the Po di Volano near Fossalta.

Enemy resistance was stiffening and he was increasing his defence of the canal barriers in the path of our advance. It was essential for the Hun to make an all out effort to keep us from cutting his last escape route to the landing stages at Zocca and Ro on the River Po. There was a large number of Huns — the remnants of 76 Panzer Corps — in the pocket East of Ferrara still to get out and cross the Po. This night was to be their last chance.

As the 1st Battalion London Irish Rifles had managed to get into Tamara, the final objective of the Brigade was the village of Saletta. The Inniskillings were to go first and push due North after capturing the Town. The Battalion was ordered to follow the Inniskillings, turn North West in Saletta and advance up the road to the village of Ruina just short of the River Po.

By early morning on the 24th., 'A' and 'B' Companies were advancing slowly but surely up the road to Ruina. The opposition became stronger and stronger until the enemy finally succeeded in halting the advance of the Companies on the Canale Fossetta, just over two thousand yards from the Po. During this advance 'B' Company demolished a 75 mm A/Tk gun with a PIAT. The main point of resistance was from the main bridge where the road crossed over the canal. Here A/Tk guns, SPs, tanks and Infantry held up all our attempts to push on or by-pass them. These enemy positions were bombed and strafed by aircraft, shelled continuously and subjected to all types of fire during the afternoon, but still the enemy held on, keeping open the escape route to the Po.

During the late afternoon, the London Irish as part of the Kangaroo Army advanced away to our left to try and reach the Po and cut off the enemy.

Before dawn on the 25th an all out assault was made on the canal and the bridge was captured intact. After that it was a swift advance up to our final objective and 'C' Company reached Ruina about 1000 hours. Soon after that the Companies occupied Borgo Mola and Gesuiti on the banks of the Po and immediately commenced searching for all the Huns who had missed the last boat across the Po. By late evening, over a hundred prisoners had been captured by the Battalion.

A few more prisoners wer rounded up the next day, but the attention of every man in the Battalion was centred on the floodbanks of the Po. Here was to be found a scene of utter devastation and destruction, proving beyond all doubt the major victory that had been achieved in destroying the enemy on the banks and to the South of the Po. Tanks, guns, armoured cars and all makes and types of cars and lorries littered the floodbanks and approaches of the Po. All the men in the Battalion had a marvellous time attempting to make some of these cars go and those that were intact provided endless amusement during the few days the Battalion stayed in its present positions.

Total victory was now achieved and the Faughs could rest on their Laurels.

„Kangaroo Army"

The 2nd Battalion the London Irish Rifles.

This is the story of the part played by the 2nd Battalion London Irish Rifles in the advance of the Eighth Army from the River Senio to the River Po, resulting in the destruction of a good part of the German Army in Italy.

During these operations, the battalion which was mounted in armoured troop carriers, known as "Kangaroos", of the 4th Hussars, formed with the 9th

Lancers a powerful mobile striking force under command of the Second Armoured Brigade.

It all really began on 9th April when after a long and dusty drive, searching all the concentration areas East of the Senio, representatives of the battalion eventually found 9th Lancers at cocktail time and "opposite numbers" were introduced to one another. During this "get — together" a tremendous barrage could be heard to the West and at 1900 hours the appearance of a thick black cloud of smoke on the horizon showed that the flamethrowers, our own included, were putting a final touch to the softening-up process of the Senio defences, before the New Zealand and the 8th Indian Divisions went into assault in this way our "engagement" to 9th Lancers and 4th Hussars took place.

The "marriage" was performed two days later just North of Lugo in territory cleared by the 8th Indian Division between the Rivers Senio and Santerno. It comprised the superimposing of first, squadrons of the 9th Lancers, and then the Kangaroos, on the company areas.

Before proceeding further with this narrative, a word should be said about the organisation within this peculiar private army. Each company, together with its allotment of eight Priest Kangaroos, lived and worked with its own Sqadron of 9th Lancers. Kangaroos were stocked with reserve ammunition and 48 hours' rations, thus making the force completely independent for a given period if necessary. In the same way Battalion HQ was mounted in eight Kangaroos, including two for medical purposes and two for reserve ammunition. At all times it moved in the closest liaison. With Tac HQ. and Armoured Regimental HQ. In addition, at various times, the force included an armoured squadron of the 4th Hussars, some flail Shermans for mine clearance, Sherman "ARCS", Churchill flame-throwing "Crocodiles" and the inevitable and priceless Sherman bull-dozers.

The force which was under command of the armour, comprised in toal over 100 major tracked vehicles. The difficulties of controlling such a force as this were readily overcome by the means of the excellent wireless communications provided in all armoured vehicles.

To return to our story, early on the 13 April, 2nd Battalion Royal Inniskilling Fusiliers broke out of the 8th Indian Division's bridge-head over the River Sonterno and advanced in a northerly direction. Following up, the Battalion crossed the Santerno to a concentration area in readiness to pass through Orders to do the latter were received at mid-day but it was not until 1330 hours that the leading squadrons were out in the open with only the enemy in front. It was found that on all occasions great difficulty was experienced in getting through the mass of vehicles which accumulated behind our own FDLs.

The line of advance was due northwards through a thousand yards wide corridor hemmed in on the right by the Santerno River and on the left by the Fossatone Canal. The country was typical of that experienced right up to the banks of the Po; perfectly flat, with orchards and farm houses at regular intervals and the occasional small village. The only variety of terrain came from the varying widths of the numerous canals and rivers.

Our advance to the R. Reno is described in the account written by the Brigade Commander. It was followed by a pause during which 56 Division on the north bank of the Reno fought westwards towards Bastia.

During this holding period of two days the only noteworthy occurence was the posting from us of R.S.M. Girvan MC who had been with the Battalion throughout its fighting existence.

56 Division having pushed on westwards opposite us, the battalion crossed the bridge which had been constructed over the River Reno early on the morning of the 17th and once again "married up" with the Tanks and Kangaroos which had gone over the previous evening. The rest of the day was chiefly noteworthy for a remarkable series of conferences which went on at Brigade HQ to decide the proper moment to unleash the Kangaroo army once again. At this time the battle for the Argenta Gap was in full swing.

At first light on the 18th the force moved forward into battle. This was an unforgettable move. Through the Orchards North of Argenta, in the narrow gap between Lake and Canal, moved a mass of armour, all passing over one bridge that had been constructed over the main water obstacle. Wrecked vehicles, equipment and enemy dead strewed the route, whilst machine-gun fire, from an Argenta already surrounded, crackled away on the left flank.

The usual difficulty was experienced in breaking through our own FDLs but by 1000 hours we were in the open and the Tanks were engaging SPs and Mk IVs. A Kangaroo was hit by an AP Shot and some trouble was experienced from Boccaleone and Consandolo on the left, neither of which had been captured, but the weight of armour and mobile Infantry was beginning to make itself felt and the advance continued with prisoners streaming in.

At about 1700 hours the tanks, who had been trying to solve the jig-saw puzzle of finding a way across the maze of ditches, discovered an intact crossing of the Fosso Benvignante and very soon they and the Infantry were over and investing the area which lay between this and the next obstacle. As it was now late in the evening, this took the enemy completely by surprise and an Officers Mess, a battery of 15 cm guns, a battery of 88 mm guns and numerous smaller AA and A.Tk pieces together with approx 200 prisoners were over-run. This all in spite of the enemy's attempts to hold us by close range firing over open sights. By the light of numerous burning houses and with a sense of complete victory, the battalion moved to its final area for the night in the vicinity of Palazzo and Coltra, having already three intact bridges over the next canal in its hands.

At 0400 hours next morning, patrols from 'G' and 'H' Companies went forward two thousand yards in an attempt to capture bridges intact over the Fossa di Porto West of Portomaggiore. All bridges were found blown but positions were established on the near bank and by first light they were joined by the never failing armour. At 1100 hours 'F' Company was ordered to go to the assistance of 56 Recce Regiment in clearing the Germans from Portomaggiore. They re-joined the Battalion late in the evening. During all these minor operations prisoners were continually being taken in groups of ten or fifteen.

It was decided during the morning to make a bridgehead over the Fossa di Porto at 1430 hours. This was done by 'G' Company to a great accompaniment of smoke, H.E. and the flame-throwing Wasps. Fourteen prisoners were taken. 'H' Company on the right followed suit, as soon as 'G' Company's bridgehead was established, and cleared the village of Porto Rotta.

The success of these operations led to the decision that the main divisional axis was to pass through Porto Rotta and the Battalion was therefore ordered to enlarge its bridgehead in order that a crossing for tank might be prepared by the Sappers. This was done at 2200 hours the same evening and was supported by timed concentrations from the Divisional Artillery. All objectives were taken by 2300 hours. Twenty enemy were captured and one SP Gun was "brewed up" by the concentrations. Our casualties were five wounded.

Under Mortar Fire, the RE bull-dozed a crossing over the two Canals comprising the Fossa di Porto and by 0200 hours on the morning of the 20th, 11 Brigade had begun to pass through in a north-westerly direction. Not until late next night was the threat removed from the left flank, thus 'H' Company was not released from guarding this flank until the morning of the 21st.

Early this same morning, the now familiar process of re-marrying up with the Tanks and Kangaroos once again took place and at 0900 hours the force moved off over the Fosso Bolognese, picking up 'H' Company on the way. The direction was Northwest towards a bridgehead which had been established, after heavy fighting by the Skins and Faughs over the Canal South of Montesanto.

Here after a short and unpleasant wait in an assembly area where the R.M.O. was wounded by a shell which burst in a tree above his Kangaroo, the forces moved through the Inniskillings going due North over very open country to the West of Voghenza. As before, some difficulty was experienced in discovering the exact locations of our own FDLs.

Continual opposition was met from well sited SPs and Tanks often situated behind groups of farm buildings, and the companies were called upon several times to de-bus and mop up enemy bazooka-men and Spandau posts. The RAF as always was putting in magnificent work, the "cab ranks" flushing or destroying several SPs and Tanks ahead of the leading squadrons.

As evening approached, resistance stiffened more and more. Fire from enemy tanks increased and 'F' Company dealt with several pockets of enemy troops, some of whome were sited up trees. Some "Uncle" targets were put down by our guns on points of resistance, but the force was now rapidly running out of the supporting range of the artillery. A definite feeling that we were out on our own with no friendly troops on either flank became very noticeable. Reports of "lots of Krauts on our right" or "can see Ted transport moving out of range on the left" began to come in.

Light now began to fail. A quick conference was held and it was decided to carry on to the final objectives. The objectives were the bridges at Cona and Quartesana.

A most unorthodox battle followed. By the light of the moon, and burning farm houses, the Tanks escorted by 'E' and 'F' Companies, attacked Quartesana and Cona respectively. Both columns were soon involved in a most chaotic battle in which tracer flew in every direction.

Quartesana, the approaches to which were continually being mortared, contained three enemy tanks, and several strong parties of bazooka-men and machine gunners. After two of our tanks had been knocked out, the enemy withdrew and escaped in the darkness over the bridge. This bridge, our objective, was captured intact.

In Cona, an even more complex battle developed. The enemy had a 15 cm gun sited 100 yards over the bridge, firing with open sights back into the bridge and down the village. It was backed up by the usual groups of machine gunners and bazooka men. At the second attempt, 'F' Company rushed the bridge, having been nobly backed up by the Tanks who were having a most uncomfortable time nosing their way round in the dark. A firm bridgehead was captured and 'H' Company were rushed up in their Kangaroos to reinforce 'F' Company. By 0100 hours on the 22nd the situation at both bridges was satisfactory. Almost 60 PW were taken during the operation besides quite a few enemy killed. Several trucks and a 15 cm gun fell into our hands, while an enemy lorry laden with artillery ammunition was hit at short range while trying to escape by one of our Tanks.

By now the Battalion was extremely tired, at least half of it having been on the go for over 72 hours. At 0600 hours on the 22nd, the Lancashire Fusiliers arrived up and relieved us. During the day, we all just slept but at 1900 hours, orders were received of a possible job as right flank protection to 11 Brigade who were doing a push that night. This task we were not called upon to perform, much to the relief of everyone. The following day was again celebrated as a day of rest and reorganisation.

At 2000 hours the battalion was warned to move in its Kangaroos to a concentration area on the right flank of a bridgehead that had been established over the Po di Volano near Fossalta. It was thought probable that the rest of the Irish Brigade would need reinforcements in their attack up through Tamara and Saletta.

After waiting in this area until 1100 hours the following morning, the battalion role was suddenly changed. The 9th Lancers were called up to rejoin us and at 1330 hours, the private army moved forward in two columns through the rest of the Irish Brigade in a movement designed to sweep the area between the River Po and the numerous canals running East from Ferrara and the Po immediately North of it. We moved forward through a maze of ditches and canals, the leading squadrons aided it is true by air reports as to where bridges were or were not blown, doing a splendid job of work in finding a way through and at the same time keeping a sharp look out for the enemy.

By 1600 hours opposition started to crop up and both 'G' and 'E' Companies did jobs of clearing enemy rear guards covered by our own Tanks. Prisoners were now being taken in large numbers. At 1800 hours reports came in over the air stating that enemy Tanks could be seen in larger numbers than before. Between then and darkness an exciting action was fought during which, 7 Mk IVs were knocked out by the 9th Lancers for the loss of only one of their own. The advance had gone so quickly that 'S' Company carriers started to come under enemy AP fire from the right flank, — a most undesirable situation

As darkness fell, the tank action continued over a wide area, while the Companies in their conspicuous Kangaroos tried their best to keep out of the armoured battle. Every farm for miles seemed to be burning and confusion seemed to reign. A decision to continue the advance by moonlight was again taken, but at 2200 hours orders were received that the general direction of the advance was to be changed a full hundred degrees. We were now, when just short of our original objective, ordered to make straight for the Po at a point NE of Ferrara where the Germans were reported to be evacuating their rearguards by pontoons.

A fire plan was laid on and by 0130 hours 'G' and 'F' Companies were feeling their way northwards with their respective tanks moving well behind. This complete change of direction during the hours of darkness was accomplished with very little difficulty in spite of the fact that we were still in contact with the enemy. As 'G' and 'F' Companies moved forward, the mass of armoured vehicles belonging to the combined armoured-infantry HQ leaguered in a field only a mile or so North of Ferrara and waited for the two Company columns to report their progress. They met with only minor opposition and by dawn were on the banks of the Po in the midst of an extraordinary collection of abandoned and burning vehicles left behind by the enemy.

They included 6 more Mark IV tanks and a large number of lorries. Many Germans who had either left it too late or could not swim were rounded up.

Thus ended the fourth and longest advance made by the Kangaroo Army. The force settles down into billets in Farms on its final battle field South of the Po and perhaps its final battlefield of this war. The total bag for the force is shown separately at the end of this narrative.

A very great feature of this series of operations was the cooperation and mutual trust established between armour and infantry, a feature without which these successes would not have been possible.

The effect on the enemy of the full weight of this cohesive force thrusting on a narrow front and disgorging Infantry rapidly at centres of strong resistance was disastrous every time the force swung into action. Due appreciation must also be made of the fact that openings and opportunities for the force to be used were made on all four occasions by hard fighting on the part of the remainder of the Irish Brigade.

Bag for the operations carried out by the
Kangaroo Army for the period 13 to 25 April 1945.

TANKS		12 brewed
		1 captured intact
		6 self brewed
ARMD CARS		2 destroyed
SPs		1 over run
		6 destroyed
		1 self destroyed
GUNS —	150 mm	4 over run
		1 destroyed
	105 mm	2 over run
		4 destroyed
	149 mm How.	2 over run
	88 mm	4 over run
		7 destroyed

	75 mm A.Tk	1 destroyed
	20 mm	2 over run
		12 destroyed
MORTARS		2 (large) destroyed
MISC —	Half tracks	1 over run
		2 destroyed
	Transport (Various)	29 destroyed and over run
	Horses	8 Captured
	Alsatians	2 Captured
	Ponies and traps	2 Captured

In addition 7 Officers, 2 MOs and 870 ORS were taken prisoner.

The Final Offensive in Italy

1st Battalion, Princess Louise's Kensington Regiment

The commencement of April found the Battailion fully deployed over the Corps front in preparation for the attack on the Senio line. On the left of the front 2 Heavy Mortar platoons from 'C' Support Group, equuipped with the new American Mortar, were in position supporting 2nd New Zealand Division. They had been given the task of neutralising known enemy positions in the area West of Cotignola. In the centre 'B' Support Group was deployed, with an additional two M.M.G. Platoons from 'D' Group under command. Their job was to help 78 Division in its part of the attack, and also to liquidate certain well known enemy positions on the Divisional front on the North bank of the Senio. On the right two Heavy Mortar platoons of "D" Support Group were to give left flank protection to 8th Indian Division, paying particular attention to the S. E. corner of the town of Lugo. A co-ordinated fire plan was worked out for all three Groups, and by 9th April the stage was completely set for the beginning of the Attack. A Battalion Control Point was established by the Commanding Officer in the central sector actually at "B" Group's Tac. HQ. on the morning of the 9th April. Promptly to time the first gun attack on the Senio position opened up, and thereafter until late at night every weapon the Battalion had deployed was firing almost continuously. The complete fire plan was shot through
D.F. fire from the Infantry of all three Divisions came tumbling over each other through the telephones wires. It was the Battalion's pride to be able to say after the attack that every call which was received was speedily and effectively answered.

The breaking of the Senio position being completed, the Battalion joined in the general surge forward towards the Santerno river. Here 8th Battalion the Argyll & Sutherland Highlanders were given the task of enlarging the bridgehead formed by 8th Indian Division over this river. Continuous support was given by 'C' Group for this operation and all platoons leapfrogged forward with the Infantry until on the 12th April a more or less static position was reached overlooking the bridges on the Sillaro river. From these positions the first observed mortar fire was put down, previous shoots in this operation having been predicted. Following a few days lull, while 56th London Division on our right caught up with 78th Division, the attack on the formidable Argenta bastion developed. 5 Northamptons were directed at the town and were supported by the M.M.G. platoons of 'B' Group from positions about 900 yards from the Cemetery. A further attack was developed by the 2nd Battalion Lancashire Fusiliers in the direction of the Fossa Marina during the evening of the 16th. Here the Mortar platoons of 'B' Group were continuously in action firing D. F. tasks on areas where the enemy was forming up for a large scale counter-attack the Lancashire Fusiliers afterwards reported that many casualties were inflicted on the enemy by this mortar fire. The 17th found the Infantry still pushing on against bitter resistance, the town of Argenta by now being cleared. Once again 'B' Group M.M.G. platoons were given the job of securing the open flank of the Infantry spearhead. Meanwhile 6th Battalion R.W.K. were ordered to break through the bridgehead over the Fossa Marina by night and to exploit forward was far as possible. A difficult night occupation was carried out by all platoons of 'C' Group, and thereafter the platoons leapfrogged forward with the leading battalions of the Brigade. A surprise counter-attack developed from the exposed left flank at Bevignante, and the Mortar platoon in position there was able to give valuable assistance to 5th Battalion Buffs in beating the attack off. The front was now extremely fluid and until 23 April all of 'C' Group platoons gave effective support to 36 Infantry Brigade in their rapid advance.

The momentum of the attack was now maintained by pressure from 38 Irish Brigade, and after a determined stand at Portomaggiore and along the Po di Volano, the enemy had only spasmodic resistance to offer. The whole of 'D' Group was continually in support of the Brigade, and many first class shoots were carried out. In particular in the area of Ruina a column of enemy vehicles was most effectively dealt with by the M.M.G. Platoons. The attack forged steadily ahead and by 25th April the flood banks of the river Po had been reached as the Division's final objective.

Throughout the whole of the operation all platoons of the Battalion were in continuous action, supporting every Battalion in the Division in turn. Some idea of the weight of fire put down by the Battalion can be gained from the following ammunition expenditure figures.

For the period 9th — 26th April.
4.2in Mortar bombs — 12,206 (approx, 136 tons of H.E.)
.303in Mk. viii. Z. — 314,750 rounds.

Operations
of 'A' Squadron with 1 R.Ir.F. Over the River Santerno
The Queen's Bays
(See Map IV).

This account describes the concentration of 'A' Squadron with the 1 R.Ir.F. in the Santerno bridgehead on the afternoon of 12 April, and their joint advance northwards on the following morning.

On the afternoon of April 12th the bridgehead over the Santerno in the area of Mondaniga was firm and 'A' Squadron was ordered to cross the river in order to exploit the success with 1 R.Ir.F. the next day. They were to be on the left of a northward advance by 38 (Irish) Brigade, while 'B' Squadron and another Battalion were to be on the right. 'A' Squadron arrived in the bridgehead approximately an hour before dark and, when the infantry arrived, formed up with their respective companies.

After dark a report was received from 38 Brigade that the Germans were withdrawing and 1 R.Ir.F. was ordered to follow up during the night. Accordingly 'C' Company on the right and 'A' Company on the left began the advance in the early hours of the morning on either side of the road running north from Mondaniga. It was arranged that the two leading troops should start in time to overtake the Companies by first light. The tanks used the road and as it was getting light reached the road junction 1500 yards to the North. Thence 2 Troop proceeded towards the North West, but 3 Troop took the turning to the right and continued North East.

After another mile 2 Troop reached the point where the road crosses the Scolo Fossatone. The bridge had been blown and since the ditch was wide, deep and full of water, there was no hope of tanks crossing until bridging equipment had been brought forward. One platoon of 'A' Company was engaging a party of Germans beyond the ditch, but the Troop could do nothing to help them so the Tp Ldr advanced north east parallel with the ditch until he approached the next track a thousand yards ahead. There, he was met by small arms fire from a group of houses by the track. He engaged these and at the same time askd on the Squadron net for some infantry to come and clear the houses. This was arranged with the Battalion Commander and consequently a platoon of 'A' Company arrived, and 6 prisoners were captured, but snipers were still firing from the cover afforded by the West bank of the ditch. The Troop Leader burst a shell from his 76 mm gun on the top of the bank which stopped the rifle fire, and a patrol which crossed shortly afterwards discovered three German dead. It was then 0900 hours, and as 'B' Company was preparing to pass through 'A' and 'C' Companies, the Tp Ldr walked over to see the fresh Company Commander.

After parting from 2 Troop, 3 Troop moved up to a house 1000 yards to the North, where 'B' Company were relieving 'C' Company.

At 0930 hours the Tp Ldrs left Company HQ to return to their tanks, having arranged to continue the advance in 15 minutes time. At 0945 hours the Tp Sgt of 2 Tp began to move forward along the line of the ditch with an infantry platoon following about 30 yards behind. They had only gone about a quarter of a mile, however, when they encountered LMG fire from some buildings called Arginello on their right flank. The platoon took cover while the troop sergeant began to engage and the troop leader, who had been supporting from the last group of houses, came forward alongside the leading tank and shot up Arginello with both small arms fire and HE until several buildings and a haystack had been set alight and a number of Germans had been seen running away. Then the Troop Leader advanced to within 50 yards of Fiume Nuova lying on the next lateral track northwards. There were signs of movement in the hamlet so the two leading tanks sprayed it with MG fire until the platoon came up and cleared the houses. Three prisoners were collected and the inhabitants reported that a further fifty Germans had left only a few minutes beforehand.

In the meantime 3 Troop on the right supported the infantry up to the line of the same lateral road. By 1130 the infantry were ready to start on the next bound and supported by 2 and 3 Troops worked up the East bank of the Scolo Fossatone.

4 Troop was in reserve at the beginning of the day, but before long it was ordered to support 'D' Company, which was to advance on the West side of the ditch. But before the tanks could cross, an Ark bridge had to be put in and for that to happen considerable work by a bulldozer was necessary. 'D' Company, therefore had to go on ahead alone. It did this at 0930 hours and the time was 1015 before the crossing was finished. Just as the bulldozer was pulling away it was fired on by a tank or SP gun from the direction of Conselice, which the Germans defended stubbornly for most of the day. The Troop leader appreciated that he could not cross except under cover of smoke, so it was arranged that the 2nd Captain's 105 mm tank, should build up a screen for 4 Troop. This manoevre was accomplished successfully, and once across the troop leader found himself again under cover of thick vineyards. After a short search he found the Company Commander who had encountered no serious difficulties in his absence. Before long 'C' Squadron passed through and began a rapid sweep up the left flank between the ditch and the railway.

By the middle of the afternoon the day's advance amounted to some 7 thousand yds. This had been achieved with extremely few casualties to the infantry and without the loss of a single tank. Yet there had been plenty of enemy machine guns which might have troubled the infantry, and bazooka men who could have hampered the tanks. The successful advance, accompanied by the capture of about 100 prisoners, was due to excellent co-operation between infantry and tanks, by which each arm eliminated the potential sources of danger to its partner.

Advance to the River Po — 24th / 25th April 1945

The 9th Lancers (See Map VII).

The following is an account of the final action fought by the "Kangaroo" Force consisting of the 9th Lancers with under command the 2nd Battalion London Irish Rifles carried in the Kangaroos of 'A' Squadron 4th Hussars, 'B' Squadron

4th Hussars in Shermans, and 'E' Battery 11 (HAC) RHA with S.P. 25 pounders. This force was used as the exploitation force for 78 Division during their advance from the River Santerno, through the Argenta Gap, up to the River Po.

The Plan.

At 1400 hours, 24th April, the Kangaroo Force which was concentrated at Fossalta was ordered to advance through the F.D.L.s of the Infantry who were held up on the general line of the Canale Naviglio and exploit westwards to Route 16 between Ferrara and the Po.

It was planned to move with two Squadron-Company groups up to start with and later on, when from the map and air photographs it appeared that the ditches allowed, to push up a third Squadron-Group.

The advance.

At 1415 hours the regimental group which consisted of 156 tracked vehicles and some 50 "A" Echelon soft skinned vehicles moved off from the concentration area and at 1500 hours the two leading Squadrons began passing through the Infantry F.D.Ls.

Almost immediately both Sqadrons reported that they were engaged with the enemy and being troubled by snipers, bazookas, Spandau fire and the odd S.P. gun.

For the first two and a half hours the advance was once again extremely slow and Squadrons were only doing about one thousand yards an hour. Once more it was evident that we would have to fight in the dark in order to reach the objective. However, from now on, the advance proceeded apace and it was evident that the enemy crust was broken. Both Squadrons reported that they were pushing on fast but there were constant reports of A. P. shot coming from the front and both flanks. 'A' Squadron on the right were picking up prisoners all the time and once again feeling embarrassed by the number. They eventually decided to leave one rifleman guarding over 50, including 3 Officers at a farmhouse and some of 'S' Company were despatched to collect them.

'B' Squadron reported that they were running into more and more A. P. and then announced that they had knocked out one Mark IV and one S. P. 75 mm in the Boara area, but they were pushing on well past the village. RHQ now halted just short of Boara and a patrol from Recce Troop reported that the bridge over the Scolo Conca and Canale Bianco at P del Diavolo were intact. They had great difficulty in getting up to the second one owing to heavy stonking. On this information 'B' Squadron 4th Hussars and 'F' Company were brought forward: they went past very quickly and got into position between 'A' and 'B' Squadrons. From now on we advanced three Squadrons up with RHQ behind 'B' Squadron 9th Lancers and 'C' Squadron and 'H' Company bringing up the rear. There was only now one hour of daylight left and all squadrons reported they were being engaged by A.P. shot from all directions — 'C' Squadron behind reporting that A.P. was coming in to them from their right rear. The odd A. P. shot was also landing in RHQ.

'B' Squadrons leading troops had now reached Malborghetto and reported three Mark IV's moving fast down the road northwards, 900 yards away. Shortly afterwards they reported that two of them were brewing and the third had got away but was hit and had smoke coming out of its tail. This third one was afterwards found holed and abandoned about two hundred yards off the road with two of the crew dead. Sgt. Edmunds hat scored a right and a left with two shots right through the turrets and Cpl. Nicholls had disposed of the third. A magnificent piece of shooting. Several of the crews were dead and Sgt. Riley from his Recce Troop Honey had a good Browning shoot at the others baling out. 'A' Squadron on the right now reported that 3rd Troop had brewed two Mark IV's and that A. P. was coming at them fast and furiously from every direction and they were heavily engaged. 'B' Squadron were heavily engaged to their front and left front and there were two 88mms firing from their left flank. At this moment they reported another two Mark IVs knocked out. For the last half hour of daylight both 'A' and 'B' Squadrons were very heavily engaged. Both Squadrons were pinned by A.P. fire and they were constantly reporting knocking out German tanks and S.P. guns. A.P. shot was flying in every direction.

Once more the 9th Lancers were engaged in a major tank versus tank battle. At last light both Squadrons were still pinned. 'B' Squadron had knocked out seven Mark IVs and two S.Ps. and 'A' Squadron three Mark IVs and two S.Ps. 'A' Squadron had one tank holed through the turret killing the gunner and slightly wounding the Troop Leader.

We were now ordered not to go on to our objectives but to concentrate where we were and be prepared to go off either NE to two crossings over the Po where there were supposed to be pontoon bridges possibly still intact or to go SW to Ferrara and contact Eight Indian Division. Two slightly different roles. The Regiment was therefore ordered to concentrate in and North of Malborghetto. This was an extremely difficult operation for 'A' Squadron and 'B' Squadron to perform. Both squadrons were still pinned. Even though it was now night, there was a full moon and the whole countryside was lit up by burning farmhouses and Mark IV tanks. Any tank movement brought a hail of A.P. shot and our tanks when they moved were silhouetted against the burning farmhouses. However by moving one tank at a time all Squadrons managed to get concentrated by midnight and all sounds of battle had died down. At this time 'A' Squadron captured intact a Mark IV tank in a farm 200 yards from their concentration area. The engine was still warm and it was doubtless one of the tanks which had been firing at them. Once again the 9th Lancers group was sitting surrounded by a ring of fire and destroyed German equipment.

We now got definite orders to proceed to the River Po at Francolino and Borgo where it was suspected that German pontoons were still in operation. It was now after midnight and this was a tall order as the regiment had already advanced 10.000 yards against heavy opposition since 1500 hours and this entailed a further advance of 5,000 yards retracing our steps part of the way. There was no information about the enemy except what we knew ourselves, i. e. that there were still a considerable number of tanks and S.P. guns to our North and it was suspected we might meet heavy opposition. We ordered therefore a patrol forward to the two objectives with a platoon of infantry leading in each case backed up by a troop of tanks, and the rest of the squadron and company backing them up about 500 yards behind. A careful fire plan was laid on with the Divisional Artillery including mediums covering the whole of both routes. This could be called on when required. At 0200 hours 'A' Squadron and 'C' Company advanced North towards Francolino and 'B' Squadron 4th Hussars and 'F' Company Northeast towards Borgo. This advance proceeded smoothly but slowly with the infantry walking the whole way and by first light both companies were established on their objectives having met only light opposition on the way and having taken a number of prisoners. There was no sign of any pontoon at either place.

On checking up in the morning we found the whole area between Ferrara and Francolino littered with German tanks, S.P. guns and equipment of all sorts. Apparently 26 Panzers were taken completely by surprise by the arrival of the Kangaroo Force. They had started to withdraw in front of us and eventually decided to stand and fight but after losing ten of their tanks by our accurate fire the remaining crews became so demoralised that they deserted their tanks and vehicles, and self-destroyed them between 2000 hours and midnight. This was confirmed by the civilians on the spot.

Not since Alamein have the 9th Lancers so beaten up a German Tank Regiment. Almost the entire tank strength of 26 Panzers must have been destroyed. Ten of their tanks were knocked out by our A.P., the remainder became so frightened that the crews of two of them baled out and gave themselves up and eleven baled out and destroyed their own tanks.

During the day and night we had advanced 15,000 yards; destroyed, captured or overrun much equipment. This amounted to:
 10 Mark IV tanks destroyed
 2 Mark IV tank captured intact
 4 S.P. guns destroyed
 11 Mark IV tanks (found abandoned and destroyed by the enemy on the
      Southern banks oft the R.Po at Francolino)
 1 S.P. gun

2 large Mortars destroyed
1 20mm gun overrun
230 prisoners taken (including 2 Officers tnd 1 M.O.)

Porto maggiore to the R.Po
The 10th Royal Hussars (PWO) (See Map VI + VII).

On the 20th April the Squadron moved to a concentration area near Portomaggiore with the rest of the Regiment. At tea-time a warning order came through, "'B' and 'C' Squadrons get ready to move". Guides were later sent back and we eventually moved up with them, at about 1830 hours and just after last light we arrived at an assembly area, a little South of the Fossa di Porto.

The big picture was roughly this — It had been decided to pass the Irish Brigade through 11th Brigade that evening. A bridgehead was to be established over the San Nicolo Canal during the night, and the advance continued on the 21st. It was essential that the Royal Engineers bridge the canal before first light, to get the armour across. The Skins were to be on the Right, supported by 'B' Squadron, 10th Royal Hussars and the Faughs on the Left. The whole attack was to be supported by a creeping barrage, as the line of the Canal had already been found to be strongly held by German infantry.

Our intention was to have two Troops, each supporting a Company across the Canal in the area Montesanto; 2nd Troop with 'B' Company on the left, 4th Troop with 'C' Company on the right. The railway line was the boundary between ourselves and the Skins, our left flank would be quite unprotected, as the Indians would not be up. Troops were allotted to Companies, 'A' — 3rd, 'B' — 2nd, 'C' — 4th and 'D' 1st.

The Faughs were doing well. By 0500 hours they had with the aid of the barrage, crossed the Canal and had both the leading Companies firm, by 0700 hours they were supported by their respective Troops; the bridgehead was now secure and about 800 yards deep. A number of prisoners had been taken, and no immediate counterattack appeared likely, but the German defensive fire was devestatingly accurate and persistent. At about 0800 hours 3rd Troop crossed the canal to join their Company who were to move out to the extreme left. A little later, 1st Troop and reserve Company moved into Montesanto itself.

The whole area was unfortunately under oberservation from each flank from high Church towers in the Villages of the district (oddly enough, almost all the towers were of a similar pattern, with higher towers than normal, making most wonderful Observation Posts in this flat rather open country). As a result it was extremely difficult to move about without a heavy 'stonk', and of course a hail of A.P. — most unpleasant!

During the morning we improved our positions, and deepened the bridgehead a little, and were fortunate to loose only one tank, which in a rapid endeavour to avoid A.P., reversed into a hollow where it stuck fast. The enemy certainly can't have been short of ammunition, for they plastered the whole area liberally and frequently; the village of Montesanto, the crossing and farms South of it receiving the greater part of it on our sector. 1st Troop pushed out 300 yards on the North flank.

At about 1400 hours the Kangaroo Force (9th Lancers and 2nd London Irish Rifles) arrived, they were to go through us and the Skins and continue the advance, unfortunately they were somewhat held up at the canal crossing, which was most uncomfortable for them and us to say the least, at last they were over into Montesanto, turned right at the Church, under the railway, through the Skins and off Towards Voghenza.

By this time the area South of the crossing had become an inferno, so Battalion and Squadron Headquarters moved quickly across into Montesanto: not a round was fired at us once we got into the village. Twenty minutes or so after, large numbers of shells of all calibres thundered down on Montesanto, followed by repeated doses every ten minutes for nearly an hour. Almost all the vehicles were hit by flying shrapnel, and the air seemed full of dust and rubble

— by happy chance nobody was killed, but the Fusiliers had a couple of men wounded. At last light the whole Squadron moved back to the other side of the Nicolo Canal and leaguered for the night.

In the meantime the Kangaroo Force, well supported by the Royal Air Force had pushed right ahead, and by 0100 hours had taken their objective (the bridges at Cona and Quartesana) and the 11th Brigade were to pass through and attack Baura and Fossalta on the 22nd.

The following morning (April 22nd) 'C' Squadron moved to a leaguer area North-West of Voghenza. It was a rest day of the 10th Royal Hussars and the Irish Brigade, but this was rudely interrupted by a "Lightning" shooting up, and indeed, bombing congested traffic approaching Voghenza — luckily we had all been off the road several hours and thus were merely spectators. In the evening on the 23rd we assembled once again at the Battalion HQ of the Faughs where we met what now seemed old friends, and were provided with the customary brew. Orders — Tamara was reported clear by 56 London Division, and so 'A' Squadron and the Skins were to move North through Tamara and on to Saletta, and there strike West for Ruina. 'B' Company would lead followed by the 4th and 3rd Troops.

We moved off at 2300 hours and all seemed to be going according to plan, except that the Fascine tanks were unable to cross the Po di Volano on account of their width, until the leading elements of 'A' Squadron approached Saletta with the Skins to find it quite definitely occupied — hand to hand fighting ensued, and subsequently two 'A' Squadron tanks were bazookaed! We were ordered to get off the road South of Tamara and hold ourselves in readiness to advance when the situation cleared a little at Saletta — we were by now feeling quite bazooka conscious!

By 0500 hours the Skins had sorted out Saletta but it was already obvious that the Germans intended to stand and fight, and at all costs keep open their escape route across the Po for the time being. At 7 o'clock in the light of day the advance continued, 'C' Company was ordered to Saletta and 1st Troop (Lieut. Elliott) brought up to support it. Just before 0745 hours 1st Troop reported that there were two horses proceeding down the road from Saletta to Tamara, which were captured en route, and put in a stable. One of them a chestnut mare, later named Gold Bridge, has been with the Regiment ever since, and been placed a couple of times in Army Race Meetings in Austria and Northern Italy.

The situation was still rather complex in Saletta to say the least, a couple of Spandaus still fired from time to time, and the ping of rifle bullets, presumably from a sniper, whistled about ones ears. 1st Troop advanced to the bridge North West of Saletta, the Krauts in this sector seemed to be pulling in their horns and the Troop did considerable execution among their fleeing remnants, but 'C' Company were heavily mortared in their move from the bridge, sustaining not a few casualties, and were naturally rather put out of their stride.

'D' Company and 4th Troop, (Lieut. Harrison) then moved up through fairly thick cover on the road to Ruina.

4th Troop reported that a tracked vehicle could be heard ahead, but apart from intermittent shelling there didn't appear to be much opposition so they were ordered to proceed with 'D' Company; this they did but lost 4 B (Cpl. Dellow) a few minutes later, knocked out by a Mark IV Special, the crew baled out and managed to get back safely. 'D' Company seemed to be able to proceed, but at the same time definitely reported that they could hear tracked vehicles, 4 A (Sgt. Moore) now advanced with them, carefully selecting a different route to that taken by 4 B, but short of the Canale Fossetta they spotted two men removing the camouflage from a 50 mm Anti-tank gun. The tank Commander ordered his driver to reverse, and immediately laid his 17 Pdr on the target, which fortunately was almost directly in front of him, and quickly fired the round he had "up the spout", within a few seconds of firing, his own gun was hit on the barrel from a different direction and rendered useless — the 50 mm too had been hit first time and never fired a round. The enemy now commenced to fire everything he had — 4th Troop's nose was in a hornet's nest to say the least, Squadron Headquarters

105 mms and 'B' Battery put down smoke and a depleted 4th Troop was retrieved. 'D' Company returned virtually unscathed! 3rd Troop now took the place of 4th Troop.

It was now obvious that the opposition ahead was rather more than a demoralized rabble, if anyone had thought that such would be the case. As the Kangaroo Force was shortly to make another advance somewhere out on our left, our duty at the moment was plainly to retain the initiative, and keep the Krauts very much occupied in holding their bridgehead.

At Squadron Headquarters we climbed the Church tower at Saletta from which we got a most wonderful view, at the same time realizing what the Germans had been able to see at Montesanto, and were still seeing — the countryside to the Po banks and beyond was stretched out before us lika a vast carpet! The whole area was continually being subjected to a hail of fire and unpleasantness from both sides. The R.A.F. were particularly aggressive during the afternoon — continually stropping up targets in houses and hedgerows, and on a number of occasions bombed the area of the Po banks, and the main road to Venice and the North on the other side of the river.

By 2030 hours light was failing and we were able to move the Squadron back to a leaguer in Saletta, where we spent a noisy but fortunately uneventful night. During the night vehicles could be heard moving back and there were a series of explosions which seemed to indicate that the Germans were pulling out. The Faughs made good progress during the hours of darkness, and by dawn it was obvious that the Bosche had packed it in, and by 10 o'clock the following morning we had reached Ruina finding all the positions abandoned and on to the Po banks without a shot being fired at us. The Faughs routed out the odd prisoner here and there, though the majority of the Germans who had not managed to withdraw across the Po had either been caught by the sweep made by the Kangaroo Force or made their way to the crossing place near Zocca, where they now found no means of crossing and were subsequently captured.

The whole area was full of destroyed tanks and guns, the river bank and surrounding country was littered with stores, ammunition, guns and other Wehrmacht equipment, much of which was still in working order, though Motor Transport had noticeably been destroyed. There was a Veterinary Hospital which had been abandoned like the thousands of horses which we found amongst these miles and miles of wreckage and stores. No wonder Tedesci had made such a fight of the last battle with all this equipment at stake! Later that day we moved to join the rest of the Regiment at Ferrara.

Within two days we knew that the entire German Army in Italy had surrendered to Field Marshal Alexander, and that for the Eighth Army, at last, the war was over.

Over the Santerno and the advance to Conselice
48th Battalion Royal Tank Regiment (See Map IV).

The final offensive in Italy was the first time that the 48th Battalion Royal Tank Regiment had had the honour to fight with 78 Division. The result of the affiliation was the successful advance from the Santerno to the Sillaro and Reno, and the bursting of the Argenta Gap. This short account deals with the former as it was the first of a series of infantry-tank night advances that were to prove so successful during the next three weeks.

The Battalion had supported 21 Brigade of 8 Indian Division across the Senio and up to the Santerno and was leaguered in Lugo when orders were received on the 11th April that the Battalion was placed in support of 36 Brigade of 78 Division. Lt.Col. P.W.D. Sturdee, commanding the Battalion, visited 36 Brigade in the afternoon and Squadrons were affiliated as follows; 'A' Squadron to 5 Buffs;, 'B' Squadron to 8 A. & SH., and 'C' Squadron to 6 RWK. Liaison was carried out during the evening and the Battalion officially came under command 78 Division that night.

Early next morning 'B' Squadron moved to 8 A. & SH. location and troops tied up with companies and both 'B' Squadron and the rest of the Battalion were at short notice to move all day.

At 1345 hours orders were issued at Argyll's HQ for operation "Archie". 'B' Squadron and 8 A. & SH. were to cross the Santerno and to attack N.W. to enlarge the bridgehead already made by 17 Indian Infantry Brigade with 12 Battalion R.T.R. and to allow 38 Irish Brigade with 2 Armoured Brigade to assemble for their break through, to the North. The attack started at 1800 hours. The objective was the S. Fossatone and the tanks started on the West side of the river. At 1930 hours the infantry were on the objective with no casualties and no resistance. A small number of PW were taken and a few enemy killed. Owing to the lack of resistance and the reports of the local civilians that the enemy had pulled back, it was decided to exploit boldly forward and capture Conselice before dawn. 6 Tp with 'B' Company therefore advanced to Zeppa Nuova about two miles to the West and 8 Tp with 'R' Company to Zeppa Superiore about 300 yards to the North. On arrival here the Squadron less 6 Tp were formed up in order of march — 8 Tp, Squadron HQ, 10 Tp, 7 Tp and 'R' Company riding on the tanks. It was now dark but artificial moonlight and the flares of a bombing programme to the North made visibility good. This task force followed by the reserve companies on foot advanced with the first objective S. Patrizio. Before starting the bridge 300 yards short of the village was shelled to discourage demolition parties and three wounded germans were found in the ditch on arrival there. Along the whole advance small pockets of enemy were rounded up and taken prisoner the total bag for the night's work was over seventy.

S. Patrizio was reached and cleared before midnight and the infantry dug in. Further orders were then asked for, and the force was ordered to seize and hold two bridges to the West of S. Patrizio. 7 Tp with one platoon went to the Northern one and 8 Tp with a platoon to the Southern one. Both met opposition from parties guarding the bridges but both bridges were intact and were secured by 0130 hours. 7 Tp shot up a bridge demolition party who tried to sneak up the canal bank and fire the prepared charges. During the night a Rhinoceros 88 mm SP gun swanned into the village hopelessly lost and out of touch with the situation and was promptly put in the bag — completely equipped and in good running order. The crew were taken prisoner, very surprised and indignant at losing their vehicle.

At 0430 hours 6 RWK arrived followed by 'C' Squadron and at first light they passed through 8 A. & SH. and 'B' Squadron to attack Conselice. By 0630 hours the infantry were within 500 yards of the outskirts of the town where they met heavy opposition from enemy in farmhouses. The Squadron Leader decided to make an armoured recce and at 0715 hours 2 Tp were ordered to move up the road running N.E. from S. Patrizio as far as the crossroads East of Conselice. They reached C. Raffi 800 yards short of this crossroads by 0825 hours with little opposition. This Tp was then halted to watch the East and N.E. approaches of the town. At about 1100 hours the Tp was ordered forward from their position to attack a house 300 yards to the North which would be taken over by the right company when cleared. The enemy were well entrenched in this house and during this small engagement the troop leaders tank was hit and brewed up killing the officer and some of the crew. The enemy attempted to salvage the tank but later were prevented by our own artillery and air. The enemy lost two anti-tank guns, their crews being killed. The shooting by these tanks was first class, as on later inspection a 6 pdr shell was founded embedded in the muzzle brake of one of the guns. Meanwhile 1 Tp in support of the left company had spent the morning shooting up enemy positions that were giving the infantry trouble. This company and Tp were under very heavy fire and the Troop Leader was wounded early in the afternoon but the Troop Sgt. reorganised the troop and continued to give the infantry support until relieved by 4 Tp. At about 1645 hours one platoon occupying a house were completely surrounded and this troop went to their assistance. The situation was restored by 1720 hours.

During the morning 'A' Squadron had moved up with the 5 Buffs to S. Patrizio. Battalion HQ had also moved with 36 Brigade HQ to farmhouses North of Zeppa. The enemy were still not clear from the area East of Conselice and North of Zeppa and 'A' Squadron had to send 1 Tp and 2 Tp out with 2 companies from the 5 Buffs to clear this area. As they moved up with the infantry on the tanks they were cheered by Battalion HQ as they passed who then felt a bit more comfortable with someone else between them and the enemy. A few PW were taken — 36 Brigade took twenty when they moved into their farmhouse.

The enemy were doggedly holding onto Conselice and a combined attack to clear the town was staged for the night 13/14 April with a troop from 'C' Squadron supporting a company of 6 RWK in an attack N.E. of the town. The attack went in at 2100 hours and by 2230 hours the area of the cemetery at the crossroads had been reached. The company of the RWK with its troop of tanks entered the town at 0400 hours. On the left 'B' Squadron and 8 A. & SH. had the task of securing the left flank while 'A' Squadron with the Buffs attacked N.W. of the town. The attack went forward slowly and surely, supported by concentrations from field and medium artillery. Just before midnight 'A' Squadron were on their objective and civilians passed on the information that the Germans had left a half an hour before. Several tanks and SP guns had been seen passing towards the West. The town was quickly occupied and there the battalion remained for two days before being called upon to take part in the next phase.

The Royal Artillery

The break out and the follow through

Headquarters Royal Artillery 78 Infantry Division

The divisional plot for 11 April was to get the Division concentrated by Brigade Groups in the vicinity of Lugo, ready for the break out. The appreciation for the divisional artillery was to get it into action so that its guns would cover the break out, individual regiments being deployed as adjacent to their own brigade 'wedding area' as possible.

Arrangements ware made for regimental recce parties to meet the BMRA to the South East of Lugo shortly after first light. Movement and recce were restricted by cratered roads and mined areas. Recce parties of 138 found themselves in the area of a local infantry battle to the immediate West of Lugo, where a stubborn party of Bosche were holding out in the cemetery although the general line of contact was on the Santerno some 2500 yards further West. This was the first of a number of occasions in this phase, when regimental recce parties, in an endeavour to get range in hand, carried out their work within small arms range of enemy rear parties.

An administrative problem which presented itself at this stage was ammunition supply. Of the 850 r.p.g. dumped for the Senio assault battle only some 600 r.p.g. had been fired. The under-expenditure was due to the speed of the advance; no repetitions had been called for, and the forecasted barrage towards the Santerno on the morning of 10 April, being no longer required, had been cancelled. There were, however, great advantages in starting off a break out battle with ammunition on the ground well forward, and it was decided to place on regiments the primary responsibility of collecting their own dumped ammunition and ferrying it forward. The decision entailed much hard work and very long hours by regimental ammunition echelons but the effort enabled the Divisional RASC to build up well forward the next Forward Ammunition Point.

The afternoon and evening of the 11th were spent on planning and re-planning, but it was not yet the moment for the Division to go into action. Meanwhile Main Division and HQRA had moved to, and were established in Lugo. It was not an ideal place as the screening effect of the high buildings made wireless communications difficult and the many street crossings made safe line laying a very slow and laborious business. Further, as was almost to be expected, the town received during the night 11th/12th a certain amount of harassing fire, one 15 cm. shell bursting in the HQRA officers' mess at 0345 hours on the 12th. It not only cut all lines between the exchange and the offices, but destroyed a prized NAAFI spirit ration, drawn only the previous afternoon.

Eventually, in the late afternoon of the 12th, 78th Division was launched, a two regimental lane barrage, with additional regiments and some medium artillery superimposed, being laid on to carry 36 Brigade through and beyond the Indian bridgehead. This fire plan simple in form, went anything but smoothly. In the first place, delays in the move of the armour to the assembly area resulted in more than one change in the time of zero, and secondly, faulty information as to the position of the troops of the Indian Infantry Brigade on the left of the one through which 38 Brigade were to pass, led unfortunately to some shells on the extreme left of the barrage falling amongst the right forward troops of the left brigade. However, progress after this sticky start was good.

From the break-out onwards the pace was so hot, the (inevitable) changes in plan so numerous, and the closeness of the final decision on top of the time to take action, that paper pracically ceased to issue from HQRA, telephone lines being correspondingly hotter and the air a good deal fuller. Much that was done in this period stood or fell by the efficiency of the line layout, and as the lines stood up to the strain, nothing failed.

A particularly hectic night was spent on the 14th/15th — our last night in Lugo. At that time Main Division, with HQRA linked to it, was alarmingly far behind RHQs — certain over-riding factors had made a move of Main Division impossible up to that time and the CRA was still of the opinion that being at almost extreme range from RHQs was a lesser evil than being divorced from Main Division. At about 2100 hours, after various counter proposals, it was finally announced from RA 5 Corps that 78 Divisional Artillery would be required to assist in a barrage being fired in support of 56 Division which was carrying out a converging attack North of the Reno in the direction of Bastia, the forecasted time of commencement being 0600 hours the next morning. It was further stated that it was hoped to have the fireplan ready at HQRA 56 Division by 2300 hours and an officer would then leave with the plan.

The CRA. realised from his own experience of the traffic congestion and circuitous tracks that the chances of this officer arriving in time were remote. The only hope of getting information to the guns in time was to phone through the controlling points of the barrage and all other orders in connection with it. This was agreed upon, but it was not until 0200 hours that HQRA 56 Division were able to start telephoning.

Speech was far from easy, hardly surprising as it came over nearly 45 miles of cable. The barrage included an irregular wheel so the controlling points were numerous, however after an exasperating 1½ hours sufficient detail was available at HQRA to redraw the barrage. Within an hour 78 Divisional Artillery regimental lanes were worked out and by 0515 hours telephoning to Regimental HQ's was completed. The barrage was fired at 0600 hours. At 0615 hours the written orders and official trace arrived from 56 Division which to the relief of everyone corresponded almost exactly with what had been drawn from the telephoned data.

The success of that night's work led us to employ on many occasions this method of passing co-ordinates of controlling points to regiments, who drew out the barrage on their own artillery boards, rather than waiting for the production of traces, which when possible followed as information, mainly for the infantry, and as checks against gross error.

The experience of the night 14th/15th also emphasised, however, the danger of excessively long communications, and it was with a great sense of relief that we heard early on the 15th of the decision to move Main Division up to within ten thousand yards of the Reno, which was then our front line.

Thereafter began a sequence which was to repeat itself three times in almost identical pattern between the Reno and the Po. There would be a check against a major defence line or obstacle, a difficult period establishing a sufficient bridgehead over the obstacle to enable mine-free lanes to be cleared or a class 40 bridge to be built across the obstacle. During this period there were often heavy calls for defensive fire. Then there would follow a major fireplan to enable a fresh brigade to enlarge the bridgehead for the armour and Kangaroos to assemble over the obstacle. Then came the launching through the troops enlarging the bridgehead of the Kangaroos Brigade, and a quick advance of 5 to 10 miles up to the next major obstacle. During these rapid advances much use was made of support by Uncle Targets on areas likely to harbour enemy SPs or towed A Tk guns. These were usually called for by the regimental commanders acting as CRA's reps and were almost always made with reference to the air photo target number.

The thrust forward of the armour was usually accompanied by a push by 36 Brigade towards some important area on the left flank. The Brigade by moving by night as well as by day balanced within the 24 hours the more rapid initial gains of the Kangaroo Brigade. Thus on 18th and 19th 36 Brigade dealt with Consandolo and Benvignante on Route 16, and on the 22nd and 23rd it thrust to the North West towards Ferrara. The effect of these diverging punches was to make the positioning of guns very difficult, for range in front of the Kangaroo Brigade could only be got at the expense of range to the flank.

Although at all times the Air OP was invaluable, the pilots would undoubtedly classify as their best days those when there was a forward surge, for during these periods they would spot and engage enemy SPs and tanks, or would be directed to seek out and destroy some hidden weapon temporarily holding up the advance. This they did with great efficiency and effectiveness.

The mobile days also brought some exciting times for the Anti-tank gunners particularly the SP troops who after a rapid gain more than once formed the rock against which German immediate counter-attacks were broken.

A sequence such as has been described took about three days to complete, the armour and Kangaroos being launched on the 18th, 21st and 24th April.

The strenuous night already described was followed, rather unexpectedly by an equally hectic afternoon and evening. As the barrage in support of 56 Division was not due to terminate until 1100 hours and 78 Division (except 11 Infantry Brigade) was for the moment stopped by the Reno until it was bridged, this in turn being not possible until Bastia was in British hands, there seemed some prospect of a comparatively quiet day. The main area of interest was clearly 11 Infantry Brigade which had been moved during the night to the North of the Reno and were in process of making arrangements to take over the sector immediately North of the Reno from 56 Division.

The artillery support for 11 Infantry Brigade was presenting a difficult problem. The general direction of the 11 Infantry Brigade advance was West. The Divisional Artillery gun areas were some 7000 yards to the South-West, and so supporting fire from this source would be towards the advancing infantry from their left front and not over their heads as is normally to be expected. There could be no question at this stage of altering the general position of the 78 Divisional Artillery guns. The route to the rear of 11 Infantry Brigade was long, circuitous and terribly congested. However, 8 Indian Divisional Artillery, in a superimposed Corps role, were in action in a position astride Route 16 some 8000 yards to the E.S.E. of Bastia, and so were suitably placed to fire on the opening line of any barrage required in support of 11 Infantry Brigade.

About mid-day it was decided that 11 Infantry Brigade must be prepared to put in an attack that night, so within a few hours available HQ's RA 56 Division and 8 Indian Division had to be contacted to settle the general methods of calling for fire. 2 AGRA, normally supporting 56 Division, was made available for medium fire instead of 1 AGRA which was in the same position as 78 Divisional Artillery and had a quiver-ful of other commitments. In the early hours of darkness 11 Brigade finding that the Kraut was withdrawing followed close on his heels, so work stopped on the fireplan and some sleep was snatched from what had threatened to be the second 'nuit blanche' running.

The 16th saw further progress by 11 Infantry Brigade beyond Bastia towards Argenta, and most important of all the completion of the 78 Division bridge over the Reno by Bastia and by early on the 17th all the divisional artillery, and also 8 Indian Divisional Artillery were in action North of the Reno, with shortened communications and behind their own infantry. A very much more satisfactory gunner situation.

On the morning of the 17th April the Skins and the Faughs advanced from the 2 LF bridgehead. They were supported by simple fireplans based on a series of concentrations which had been laid on at very short notice by the regimental commanders. The brigade thrusts soon diverged far from the 'direct' advance and quick barrages had to be laid on to meet local requirements.

From the firing of Fire Plan MURPHY at 1100 hours on the 17th there was an increasing rate of progress and by that evening the Argenta defences were prized open. By the 25th the Divisional Artillery was in action within some 7000 yards of the Po covering the last mopping up operations of the Division, and so it was the last day the divisional artillery fought in support of its own division, but just as the divisional artillery were fully involved in the Final Offensive from the earliest planning stage of the assault, so the divisional artillery was in the battle for an extra 36 hours. This was to support our friends of the 8th Indian Division by being in a position to cover their advance, from their bridgehead, to the NNW of Ferrara, along Route 16, until such time as the 8 Indian Divisional Artillery were across the river. Accordingly positions were reconnoitred within 1500 yards of the Polesella bend and occupied by an early hour on the 26th. As the remnants of the Hun army defeated South of the Po made no attempt to dispute the advance of the Indians we were not called on except for 138 Field which fired fairly early on 26 April one Uncle Target scale one at a few Huns, to help them on their way North. The final cease fire came at 1100 hours on the 27th April.

Glasgow Yeomen try out their new S.Ps.

64 (Glasgow Yeomanry) Anti Tank Regiment R.A.

64th Anti-Tank Regiment entered the final offensive in Italy in an adventurous spirit. It was felt that with the newly acquired SP guns the Regiment would be able to play a more pugnacious role in the battle than hitherto.

These expectations were fully justified. By the three weeks campaign, each of the three new M 10 Troops, as well as the ready-made SP Battery (209 Battery) which had come to the Regiment, had a crop of exciting actions to their credit.

256 Battery's 'H' Troop was one of the first to be involved when, in the very early stages of the offensive, they were largely responsible for the defence of a vital canal bridge-head against determined counter attacks. On April 13th the Troop was supporting 36 Brigade's drive on Conselice, and was teamed up with two troops of the Recce Regiment to exploit a footing which the Argylls had secured over one of the numerous canals in the district.

Having advanced some thousand yards this force reached a junction from which roads branched North and West. A strong point was established here with 'H' Troop's two M 10s and a number of armoured cars, while one troop of Recce probed up the road northwards towards a cluster of four houses some eight hundred yards away. Everything went without incident until the armoured cars were well up to the houses, when they came under heavy Spandau fire from all round, and were forced to pull back to a farmhouse about four hundred yards away.

Answering a call for help one of the M 10s made its way across country up to this farmhouse and nosed into a fire position from which it could engage the troublesome casas. They did not remain troublesome much longer. A bit of particularly good shooting effectively obliterated all four houses — and surely most of the occupants — in turn from the right. The last two were set on fire.

Hard on this success, however, came reports from the Recce that an enemy tank (alleged as usual to be a Tiger) was coming down the road. This was quickly followed by further reports of tanks on either flank with accompanying infantry. Accordingly it was decided to pull back to the original strong point. The M 10 found itself a cosy little hull down a hollow and everyone sat tight waiting for developments.

There was not long to wait. German infantry, apparently a strong patrol, appeared coming through an orchard to the West of the position, and, in the middle of this excitment an enemy SP gun suddenly opened up from some incredibly short range to pump four random shots into the area of the strong point. The infantry were effectively repulsed, but the SP gun fared better, one of its shots having luckily made contact with one of the two M 10s and destroyed the sight bracket.

Reports of more tanks in the vicinity coincided with orders from Brigade that the position would be held at all costs.

The expected attack eventually came in from the West in something like two company strength. They came down the ditches on either side of the road and in open order through the orchard. DF was out of the question owing to the close proximity of the enemy and so the defenders had to rely entirely on their own resources. They opened up with everything they had — rifles, Brens, 50 cal. Brownings and all the assorted musketry of the Recce. After a tough tussle the enemy withdrew, in considerably less strength than he had set out.

Orders had been carried out. The position had been held. At dusk a two battalion attack passed through to bring relief to the gallant defenders.

Counter attack at Benvignante

138 Field Regiment RA

The main defences of the Argenta Gap had just been breached. 6 RWK were fighting for Boccaleone, 8 A. & SH. for Consandolo and 5 Buffs were in reserve.

The final rout of the Hun was beginning and he was fighting desperately wherever he could stand.

Route 16, a fine road running North from Argenta, was the main enemy axis on this sector.

On the afternoon of 18 April a Task Force, consisting of 5 Buffs with under command one Squadron Churchills, one Mobile Bridging Unit, one Company REs and Support Group Mortars, was ordered to proceed up Route 16 and to seize and hold all bridges.

5 Buffs were to marry up with the Tanks a few hundred yards East of Boccaleone at first dark. This was accomplished without exceptional incidents, the Battalion having been lifted in 3-tonners to a remarkably forward debussing area. The intended route via Boccaleone was impassable since 6 RWK were still fighting for part of the village and a liberal mixture of our own and enemy artillery appeared to be coming down from everywhere. The only alternative was cross country and, in spite of encounters with apparently impassable bogs, ditches and dykes, the column proceeded into the night.

Things went well — by last dark about 100 extremely surprised Kraut and a few guns and vehicles had been picked up from various L. of C. houses en route and the two leading companies had reached Benvignante where they were meeting some opposition.

Eight miles of Route 16 were now held intact.

The C. O. decidet to consolidate at Benvignante. Two companies concentrated in farms to the North of the small village and one Company in the village. Daylight revealed various vehicle and enemy tank tracks all too fresh to be treated lightly. It was flat open country and lightly wooded, and since we were open on all flanks the C.O. wisely decided to establish Tac BHQ with the Company in the village. Local small arms exchanges encouraged them not to waste time in the process!

Whilst we were still sorting ourselves out, the local Company Commander suddenly reported on his 18 set that 100 Kraut and 2 tanks were approaching through the trees about 200 to 300 yards away to the West, and asked for an artillery FOO. The only FOO was already deployed with the most northerly company and could see nothing of our local excitement. Fortunately, the guns were able to provide 2 of the 15 DF tasks which ringed the village but it left much to be desired since Field Artillery Regiments were in the process of moving by batteries and, for some mysterious reason, the remote control of 359 Battery Commander's wireless set chose this particular period to start misbehaving.

The situation developed rapidly. The enemy was already established in some houses on the opposite side of the road and was firing practically point blank with an SP through an archway from one of the houses, at the group of buildings housing part of the Company and Tac BHQ, and was inflicting considerable casualties. The most Northerly Company now reported more enemy and two more tanks approaching from the North West. At this stage a Medium FOO appeared at BHQ, having parked his vehicle — a Churchill — in the road outside, and enquired whether there was anything he could do! He was extremely rapidly briefed and set off round the houses for an OP. By some miracle (or perhaps just quiet efficiency) he produced the accurate fire of two Medium Regiments, and, working in conjunction with the Field FOO, the results were both deadly and decisive. The Hun was put to rout in screaming panic. Incidentally, whilst the excitement was cooling off, two of the Gnr Drivers went out to the back of the house and returned with two more very frightened Kraut who had been hugging a slit trench in the yard.

Rum and cha rounded off a touchy 1½ hours, and soon the visitors began to arrive. Next afternoon 6 Armoured Division flooded through, and in a matter or minutes, this outpost became a base area.

The battle had moved on!

In Action against the Argenta Gap defences
17th Field Regiment R.A.

The Regiment had a particularly busy time on 17 April and during the morning of 18 April.

The plan was for the Irish Brigade to pass through the 11 Brigade bridgehead over the Fossa Marina and seal off Argenta from the North. It was a difficult move to get the Regiment across the newly made Reno Bridge by night, but by shortly after first light all three batteries were in position 3000 yards S.E. of Argenta. With the FDL's only 1500 yards away dust inevitably attracted attention and the Regiment recieved several stonks. Luckily however casualties were light.

At about 1100 hours the 'Skins' started moving through the 2 LF and pushed forward supported by a series of concentrations from the Divisional Artillery assisted by the guns of the 8th Indian Division. As soon as they got going the OPs of 10 Battery did a lot of observed shooting and kept it up right up to dusk.

On the right 26 Battery laid on a fireplan 'Murphy' (named in honour of the Battalion Commander) to get the 'Faughs' going. It consisted of 5 concentrations and had in the end to be repeated again as unforseen obstacles held up the armour. 26 Battery did a lot of observed shooting and the air got pretty warm at times to put it mildly.

By the late afternoon both Battalions had made good progress but the Brigade Commander decided that the 'Faughs' should push on again that night and fireplan 'Belfast' was laid on. It consisted of a barrage with a two regimental lane — one Field Regiment superimposed 200^x and one Medium Regiment superimposed 400^x.

Some anxiety was felt about 56 Division on the right but luckily no trouble was experienced in contacting the Battalion Commander of the Battalion next door. Just as well too because they were proposing to walk into 'Belfast'. The danger was obviated by cutting a slice out of the bottom of the barrage and a somewhat anxious Regimental Commander breathed a sigh of relief.

The Barrage proved a great success and to use 'B' Company Commanders words "we strolled to our objective under cover of the barrage". 'B' and 'C' Companies had no difficulty in reaching their objective and consolidating (It is said that 'B' Company found that their minesweepers reacted to some buried champagne). Casualties were light ('B' Company one only) and 'D' Company captured two tanks. The ground was well covered with craters from the barrage and the Hun was obviously pretty rattled judging by the amount of equipment hastily thrown aside.

Although battered the Hun was game to put in a series of counter attacks at first light, 18 April. These were strongly discouraged by 5 'U' Tgts and came to nothing. From then on he made desperate efforts to get his armour away but OPs had a good view and pinned him down. Up to noon OPs did a lot of shooting at tanks, very ably assisted by the Mediums on a direct wireless link, and one OP claimed three.

So ended that phase for the Irish Brigade — the back of the position was broken and the time was ripe for loosing the LIR in their Kangaroos. The Regiment had had a pretty strenuous time since midnight 16 April but all were braced by the knowledge that we were then well under way for the Po.

Extract from a diary of 132 Field Regiment 16 — 19 April
132 (Welsh) Feld Regiment R.A.

16 April

Dawn saw 11 Brigade in the lead, advancing astride the railway with 1 Surreys on the right and 5 Northamptons on the left. Progress was slow and there were a great many calls for fire. The ammunition problem continued to tax us. An L.O. was sent to 8 Indian Division with a set on the 'H' Net and recce parties who had been straining at the leash for some hours were given the 'off' before noon.

The route round by the right hand bridge was a long one and much blocked by 8 Indian Divisional Artillery. It was noticeable throughout this advance that traffic control was excellent on divisional axes, but as soon as one got on a road that was common to elements of two divisions it virtually ceased to exist.

The new gun area, San Biagio North of Bastia, was the most damaged area we had seen so far in the advance. The whole area had been most accurately covered by anti-personnel bombs and practically all the roads were cratered by the heavies.

This made it most difficult to get about in M.T. and the recce took a very long time. Meanwhile the guns were very busy firing 'U' targets and observed shoots for the Air O.P. Orders were received that the guns were not to move before the completion of a fire plan due to be fired at 2000 hours to help leading elements of 11 Brigade to clear up to the Eastern flank of Argenta. Meanwhile three further batteries (50 Battery [24 Field Regiment], 214 HAA Battery, and 'Q' Radar Battery), had attached themselves to the regiment to enable them to communicate with the outside world by line and to a varying extent for operational purposes. These kept the recce parties very busy indeed.

Fortunately the Bastia bridge was completed by 1900 hours and all three batteries were able to move forward between 2130 and 2300 hours. As soon as the trails were on the ground the guns were firing again, for by this time the Lancashire Fusiliers had gone through the Surreys on the right and were closing up to the Fossa Marina. A series of D.F. tasks had been arranged along this obstacle and fire was called for on them at short intervals throughout the remainder of the night.

17 April

Had the German commander been able to lay his hand on a reserve of, say, one full strength regiment, there is little doubt that the Fossa Marina line would have proved a very formidable obstacle. As it was 42 Jager and 362 Infantry Divisions were now at the end of their tether and on the night of the 16th elements of 29 Panzer Grenadiers, his last complete formation in reserve, were hastily rushed up to the Fossa Marina. These troops, who had come from the Po did not know the terrain and few of them saw it in daylight. They did, however, know that they were likely to be atacked. Their dugouts were excellent, but the first concentration fell before the relief was complete and the enemy commanders on the spot promptly ordered everyone to keep his head up in anticipation of a following wave of British Infantry. The L.Fs did not attempt to cross before there had been several more concentrations, which daylight revealed to have done enormous damage to the enemy, compared with the disappointing results in the way of dead Huns that were normally the case after a barrage.

The L.Fs were able to establish a bridgehead over the Fossa Marina before dawn but this was very heavily counter attacked by fire in the early hours of the 17th.

It was a busy day for the guns but our infantry made little progress and Argenta remained his, though elements of the Irish Brigade passed through the L.Fs bridgehead and threatened to outflank the town. By evening the Inniskillings had crossed Route 16 North of the town but S. Antonio was still a thorn in our side and some stouthearted enemy actually counterattacked southwards from there early the following morning. The Argenta Gap was cracked but not yet open. Argenta itself was cleared in the evening.

18 April

11 Brigade HQ together with Tac RHQ moved into Argenta in the morning. The battle North of the Fossa was getting fluid. There were many reports of counter attacks supported by tanks and SP guns, but all were repulsed without difficulty. About 1000 hours the recce parties crossed the Fossa and found a tank battle in progress in the square in which they had been ordered to recce. In this they took no very gallant part, but had their share of excitement as the ruined farm at which it had been decided to establish RHQ was found to be "the target for today" for a troop of 88 mms.

Considering the power of the Division's punch which on this day reached its full momentum (36 Brigade had captured Boccaleone and were well on their way to Consandolo) it was surprising how much harassing fire the enemy was able to maintain in the area of the original Fossa bridgehead. They were no doubt largely SP guns, handled well and boldly, but the accuracy of the little 'C.B.' fire they put down on the first British guns to fire from positions North of the Fossa was remarkable.

The guns moved up from S. Biagio and were in action shortly after dark, thanks to good digging with only one casualty.

Meanwhile the Kangaroo Force followed up by 9 Lancers and the L.I.R. had made the most spectacular advance of the battle to date. By midnight they were reported right up on the Fossa de Porto North of Consandolo and West of Porto Maggiore. The enemy was given no rest and it was decided to exploit this success immediately. A sleepless night was spent planning at 11 Brigade HQ and recce parties were on the move again by 0415 hours with the L.Fs and E Surreys who were directed to consolidate the success gained by the 9 Lancers.

19 April

The whole regiment was on the move the following morning by 0700 hours through country which showed little signs of battle except for tank tracks and for 5 miles we saw no human military life whatever. Just as the guns were coming into action, however, the cornfields by the Fosso Benvignante came to life and one Battery recce party captured 5 offrs and 53 O.Rs., mostly from the artillery of 42 Jager Division, who were more than ready to give themselves up.

The Argenta Gap was now well and truly broken, through, it was not possible to maintain the impetus of the advance through country more thoroughly intersected by water obstacles than any we had met.

Conclusion

Argenta was not an artillery battle: it was an infantry slogging match. Artillery battles require much preparation and there was no time for that at Argenta where the key to success lay in hitting the already disorganised enemy hard and repeatedly before he had the chance to regain his balance. It is, however, probable that the number of rounds of 25 pdr ammunition fired in the Argenta Gap exceeded the number of rounds of S.A.A. This would seem to indicate that a great deal of the slogging was done by the guns. There was no elaborate fire plan and the value of the support given was enhanced enormously by the accuracy of the maps combined with the fact that the enemy was confined in his choice of positions to the features clearly marked on them. The pre-arranged 'U' targets were also of great assistance and resulted in the saving of a great deal of time in the encoding and decoding of map references.

Capture of the bridge at Cona
11th (H.A.C.) Regiment R.H.A.

The 9 L group concentrated near Montesanto to pass through 38 Brigade and 10 H. We arrived in the area about 1000 hours on 21 April and had to sit around untill well after mid-day, tanks, Kangaroos and the Battery all huddled far too close together for comfort. Our left flank was very exposed and a certain amount of Spandau and rifle-fire kept heads down, while an enemy battery seemed to have our location well registered. In view of the delay, the BC ordered the Battery into action near the concentration area, where they suffered some most unpleasant shelling and air-bursting and L/Bdr. Duckworth was most unfortunately killed.

Shortly after, the armour moved slowly on, 'B' Squadron right and 'C' Squadron left. Their objectives were Quartesana and Cona respectively, 6 miles away as the crow flies and only the same number of hours of daylight left. However, they pushed on in the face of fairly heavy shelling. Two 'U' targets ordered by the BC on built-up areas on the right flank were very effective and a prominent tower was hit three times, which added to the effect and greatly impressed the cavalry. Both Squadrons reached Gualdo area towards last light and the left-hand OP could see Cona, until enemy shelling blinded his observation with smoke and dust. Here there was a bit of a defile and 'C' Squadron had to come righthanded into the road to avoid an intricate canal system. When they were through, it was too dark to deploy and they were ordered to carry on in the moonlight as best they could. It was a most exciting ride, with houses set on fire all along the route, a certain amount of rather wild AP fire from the enemy, and the constant fear of bazooka-men. 9 L RHQ closely pursued the leading Squadrons and Tac Brigade were also mixed up in the tail. Both objectives were captured about the same time, an hour or so after dark, and the LIR, dismounting from their Kangaroos, secured the bridge at Cona intact. A Troop was sent over with the infantry and over-ran a 150 mm firing at point-blank range and the usual ring of DFs was laid on. Enemy tanks were heard driving away during the night and some HF was fired to speed them on their way. The night was otherwise quiet except for a 210 mm firing into the bridge area at regular intervals from somewhere near the Pc.

The exercise was very fatiguing but it proved a lesson that we had been rather slow to learn earlier in the battle, viz that an extra push after last light could produce surprisingly successful results and save possibly two or three days delay, if it was a matter of securing a bridge. Opposition was never so strong that the armour could not deal with it themselves and OPs rarely used anything less than a crash from the Battery on the few occasions when they felt they could help with the guns, using them more for morale effect than against a specific target. This day was typical of the other break-through days, only more exciting and brilliant, if anything, than others.

The Royal Engineers

The advance from the Senio to the Po

Royal Engineers 78 Division

March had been a month of preparation. Days were spent in experiment, demolition of floodbanks, use of assault equipment, rapid bridging methods-all presented problems that were studied and re-studied until the questions they posed were answered and the answers proved. Early April saw the tension increased. There were speculations about the weather, about the enemy's morale, about his intentions. One thing alone was sure, this was to be the last offensive.

78th Division did not take part in the attack that breached the Senio line. Their role was to be the classic one of exploitation. On April 10th — the day after the attack had begun 237 (H) Field Company built a 60 ft Bailey bridge across the Senio. That day and the next, the Division poured across the river into the concentration areas around Lugo. For the sappers there were craters to be repaired and mines to be lifted. At this time was instituted a custom by which a Sapper officer each day made an air reconnaissance of the ground to be covered by the days advance. Extremely valuable information on demolitions and obstacles was obtained in this way and enabled a comprehensive plan to be made for the days work.

On the night of the 11th April, the Santerno was crossed and 78th Division passed through into the bridgehead established by Indian and New Zealand troops. The break-out was made by two brigades — 36 Brigade attacking Westwards towards the Torrento Sillaro while covering the flank of 38 (Irish) Brigade's main drive North along the line of the Fiume Santerno. Good progress was made by the Infantry and tanks, and the sapper companies supporting them repaired craters and established the brigade axis. The situation was frequently confused. One sergeant from 256 Field Company, removing charges from a captured bridge was justifiably surprised when a bridge was blown up only 50 yards away, and far behind the leading troops.

On the 13th April, 214 Field Company — with 'E' Assault Squadron of 'A' Assault Regiment attached to them — made a Arc crossing of the Scolo Fossatone. Maintenance of roads — for Up traffic, Down traffic and tanks — became as it was to remain — the main problem. Several occasions saw sapper units being shelled, casualties fortunately were light, but they included a hit on a bulldozer that wounded two operators and immobilised the machine.

On the 14th, 36 Brigade was on the Sillaro and 38 Brigade was on the Reno. 214 Field Company spanned the partly demolished bridge over the Scolo Conselice with two 50 ft Bailey bridges, after an Arc had enabled the leading tanks to cross before it slipped askew. A reconnaissance of the Reno was attempted but was prevented by enemy machine gun fire.

The advance had been so rapid that many minefields were over-run still with their marking signs on and wire around them. In one case, Flails were used to make a track to the rivers edge, but this track was not developed.

The following evening after several other sites had been chosen and then cancelled, bridging began alongside the railway bridge, and by afternoon of the 16th a 110 ft bridge with its long and difficult approaches was opened to traffic.

Meanwhile, the 11 Brigade had crossed the Reno lower down in the 56 Division area and had begun to attack on their left. The reconnaissance flight these days looked down on an area that was bounded on the West by the Reno and its swamps, on the East by Lake Commacchio and the marshes that fringed it. Across the narrow strip of land between them — some four miles wide — in the ruins of Argenta and along the tank-proof Fosso Marina, the enemy had prepared his major line of resistance. By the 17th against fierce and determined opposition, this line was broken and Argenta was ours. Flail tanks had made a gap in the minefields, enabling an Arc crossing of the Fosso to be made. The next day, 237 Field Company replaced this Arc by a small Bailey bridge.

256 Field Company were also supporting 11 Brigade in their attack. The truck in which their O.C. and another officer were travelling, was blown up on a mine, but neither were wounded and each insisted on remaining at his post. This company began to open the roads trough the much damaged Argenta.

These were hectic days, the situation changed so rapidly that it was seldom possible to plan in advance with any certainty. Plans were formulated, effected and countermanded (Didn't you know? Its all been changed). For the sappers particularly, the administration problems raised were vast and never ending. Simple matters, like marrying a bulldozer to its transporter or getting diesel to some mechanical equipment that was far from its parent unit — all such things had to be foreseen and catered for. If, perhaps, these problems fell particularly hardly on 281 Field Park Company, there could have been no unit more competent to cope with them.

By the 19th out troops were meeting strong resistance along the line of the Fossa di Porto. The enemy had committed the 29th Panzer Grenadier Division in a last effort to stabilise a line somewhere, somehow. But by nightfall, Infantry were across and still advancing. 214 Field Company bulldozed the crossing of the twin canals — during which operation the officer in charge was wounded.

In the night, bombs were dropped on the area of HQRE and 281 Field Park Company.

A great amount of work was still being done by the R.E. to open up roads and keep them operating. On the 20th, 256 Field Company built a 70 ft bridge South of Portomaggiore, and the next day — after having been held up by a most insistent pocket of enemy — built a 100 ft bridge in that town. 237 Field Company bulldozed a crossing of the San Nicolo Canal, enabling 38 Brigade to take up the chase. 214 Field Company, supporting 2nd Armoured Brigade, built an 80 ft bridge at Runco after they, too had been held up by a pocket of enemy near the interdivisional boundary. This company also filled in several craters in Quartesana during the night.

The 22nd saw the Division established on the Po di Volano. A few infantry crossed the river in assault boats, and behind this very slender bridgehead, the sappers began to build a large bridge which was necessary. Work was begun by 256 Field Company shortly before dawn on the 23rd and the bridge — a 130 ft Double/Double Bailey — was completed by 237 Field Company by nightfall. For reasons that must remain for ever untold, it was christened "Lucky Diver" bridge. Despite the nearness to the enemy positions, there was relatively little shelling and no casualties.

The next day saw an Indian summer of German resistance as they tried vainly to get their troops back behind the Po. By dawn on the 25th all resistance had been smashed, the Po reached all along the Divisional front, and the area thouroughly swept for the last enemy in hiding. Companies opened the axes and the tank track up to the Po. 256 Field Company constructed a Down route over the Po di Volano, building for this purpose a 120 ft bridge; the central 80 ft being Double/Double with 20 ft at each end Double/Single. As a corollary to the "Lucky Diver" bridge this was christened "Happy Mermaid".

78th Division now passed into 5 Corps reserve.

On the afternoon of the 25th, a company passed beneath the command of each neighbouring Division; 237 Field Company going to 8th Indian and 214 Field Company to 56 Division. Their specific job was to help in the assault crossing of the Po; but since this was unopposed 214th Field Company found their primary task was road maintenance. Subsequently, both they and 237 Field Company operated rafts across the Po.

256 Field Company meanwhile began to collect together all the enemy bridging equipment left by the river side. Later, an improvised bridge, Bailey on German pontoons — was to be built. On the 29th, both 214 and 237 Field Companies returned to the Divisional area and the C.R.E's command.

Thus, three weeks after the opening of the offensive, the Division was encamped in an area that was strewn with destroyed enemy tanks, guns and transport. This was a sight to which our troops had looked forward throughout the long Winter in the Appenines, and the early spring in Romagna; for this was the destruction of the enemy's force. This was Victory.

SOME EXTRACTS FROM UNIT WAR DIARIES

Royal Engineers 78 Division

Strange behaviour on the Po di Volano

'The atmosphere was peaceful, but the infantry were crawling around on their stomachs.'

(237 Fd.Coy., R.E. 23rd April).

I always knew that stuff would come useful,

'Difficulty in obtaining cutting tools entailed use of G. 1098 equipment.'

(237 Fd.Coy., R.E. 2nd April).

The tribulations of a Company Commander.

'The O.C. was sent to the wrong location of 11 Bde. This is the third time he has been wrongly directed by higher formations in the last 7 days. First time he blew up on a mine. Second time he underwent Spandau fire. This time, since he was near Bde, he suffered only inconvenience and dust.'

(256 Fd.Coy., R.E. 22nd April).

Some little known ghosts.

'A strange section of tippers attached themselves to us, but before anything could be done they disappeared as mysteriously as they had come.'

(237 Fd.Coy., R.E. 16th April).

THE END

SITUATION AS AT 1200 HRS 9 APR '45

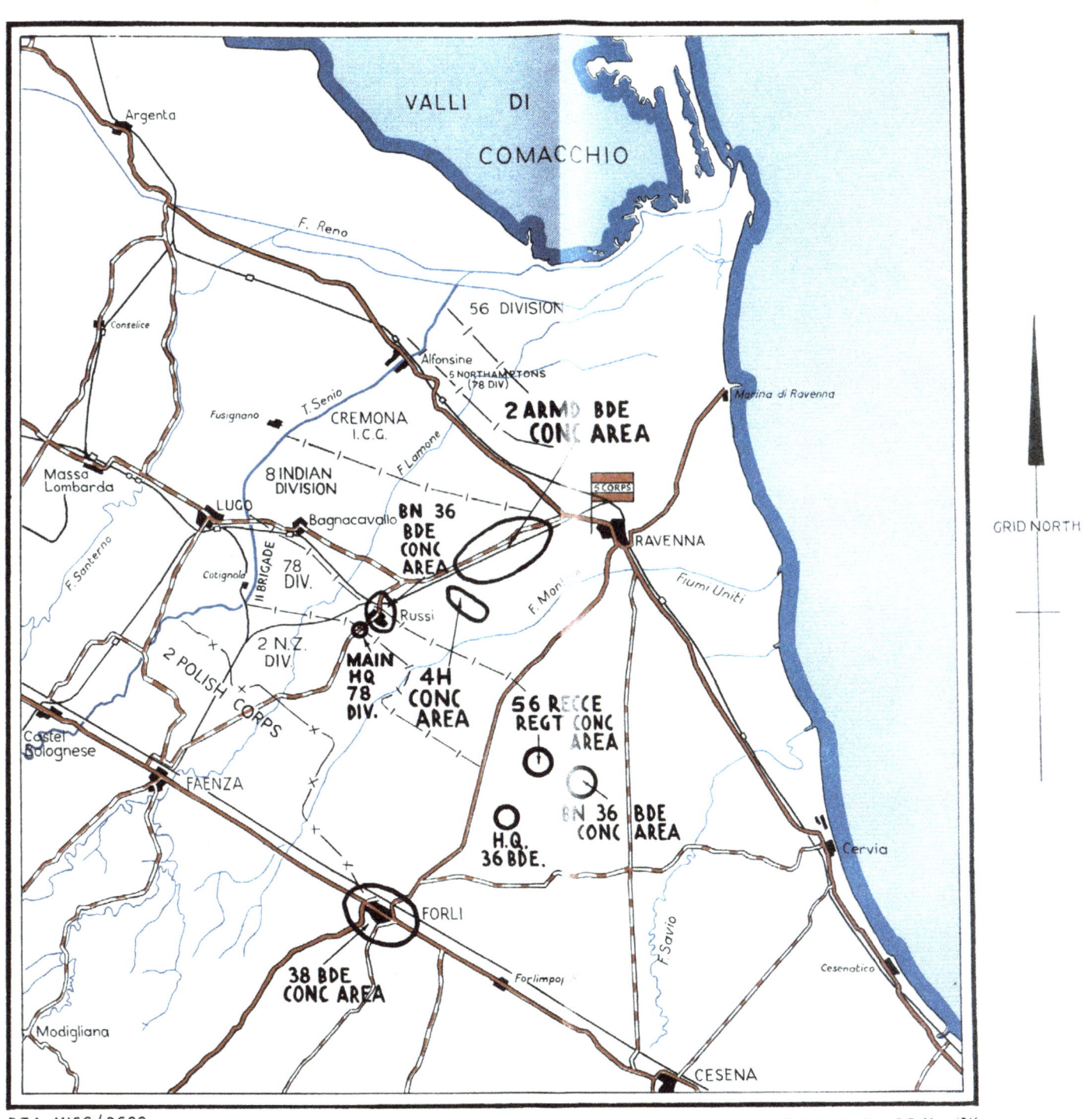

SITUATION AS AT 1800 HRS 10 APR '45

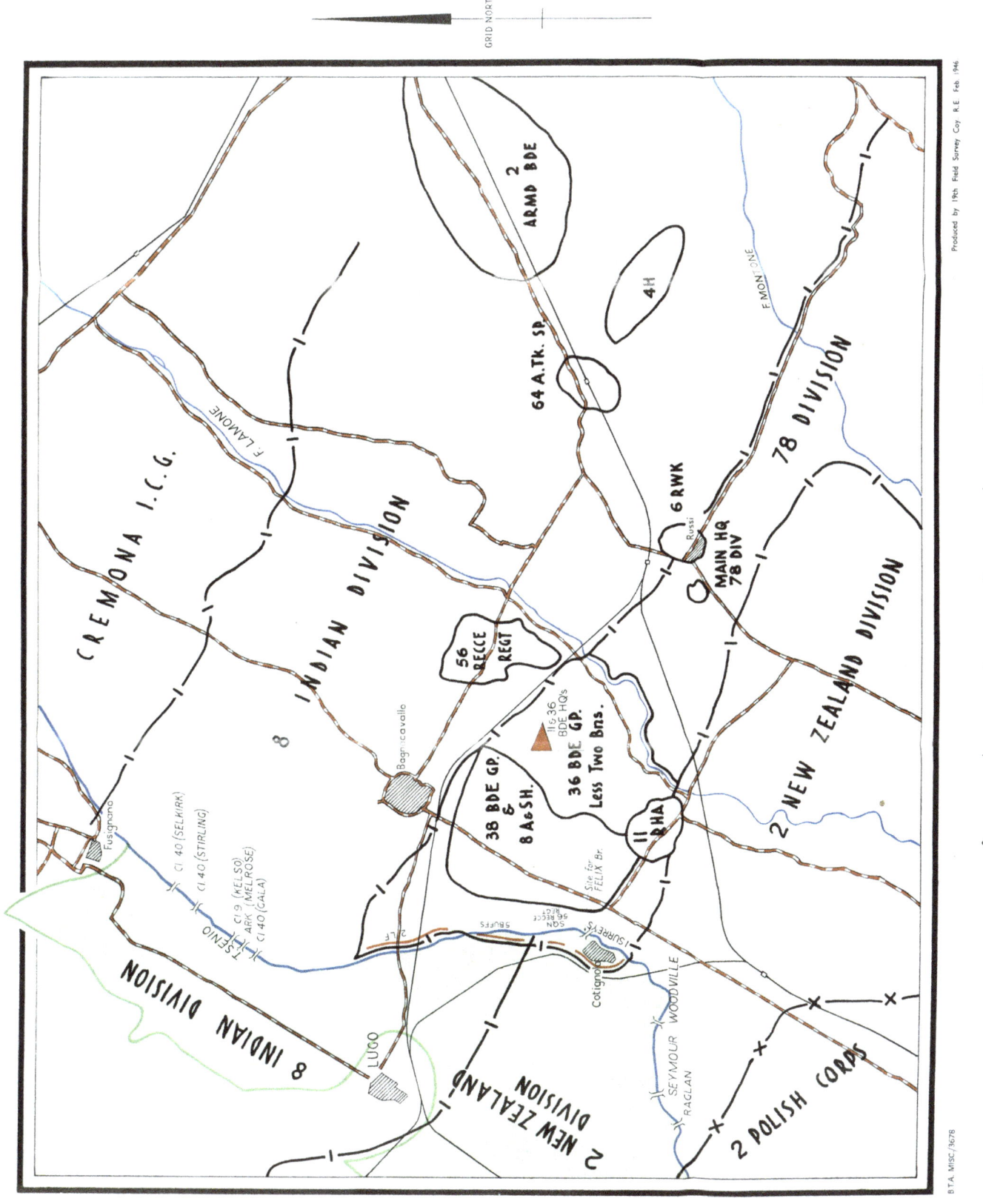

SITUATION AS AT 1800 HRS 11 APR '45

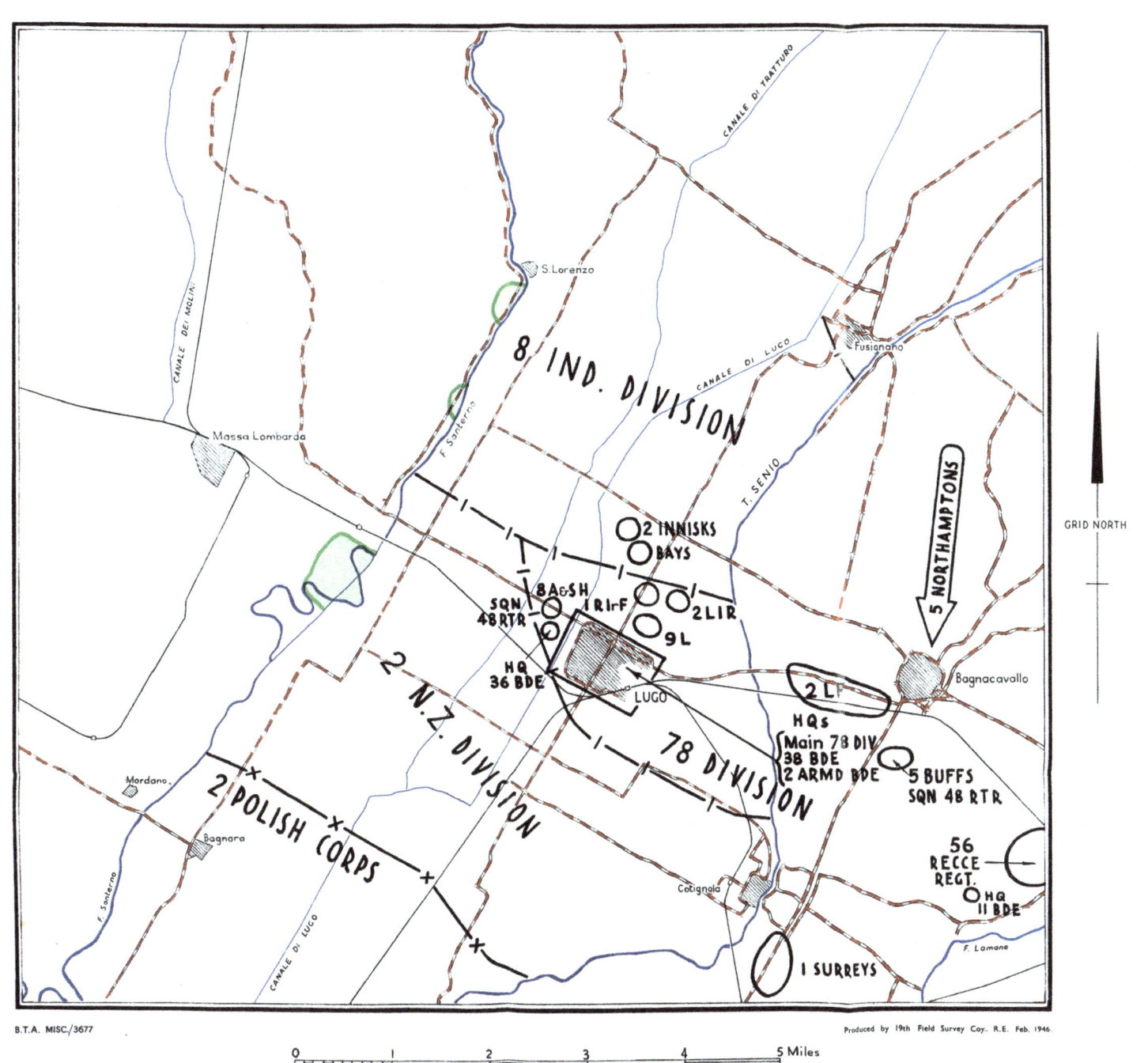

SHOWING ADVANCE 12-14 APR '45

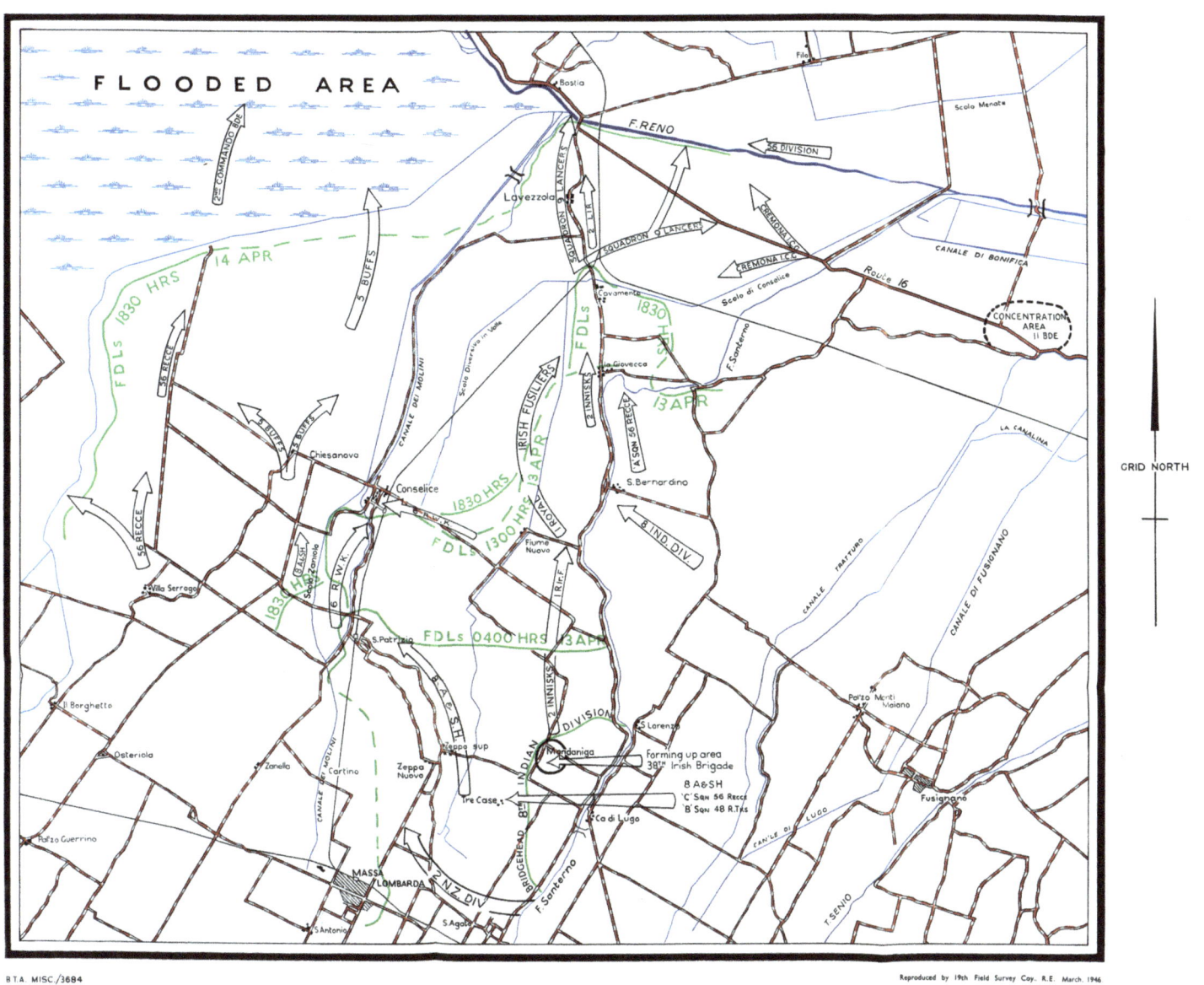

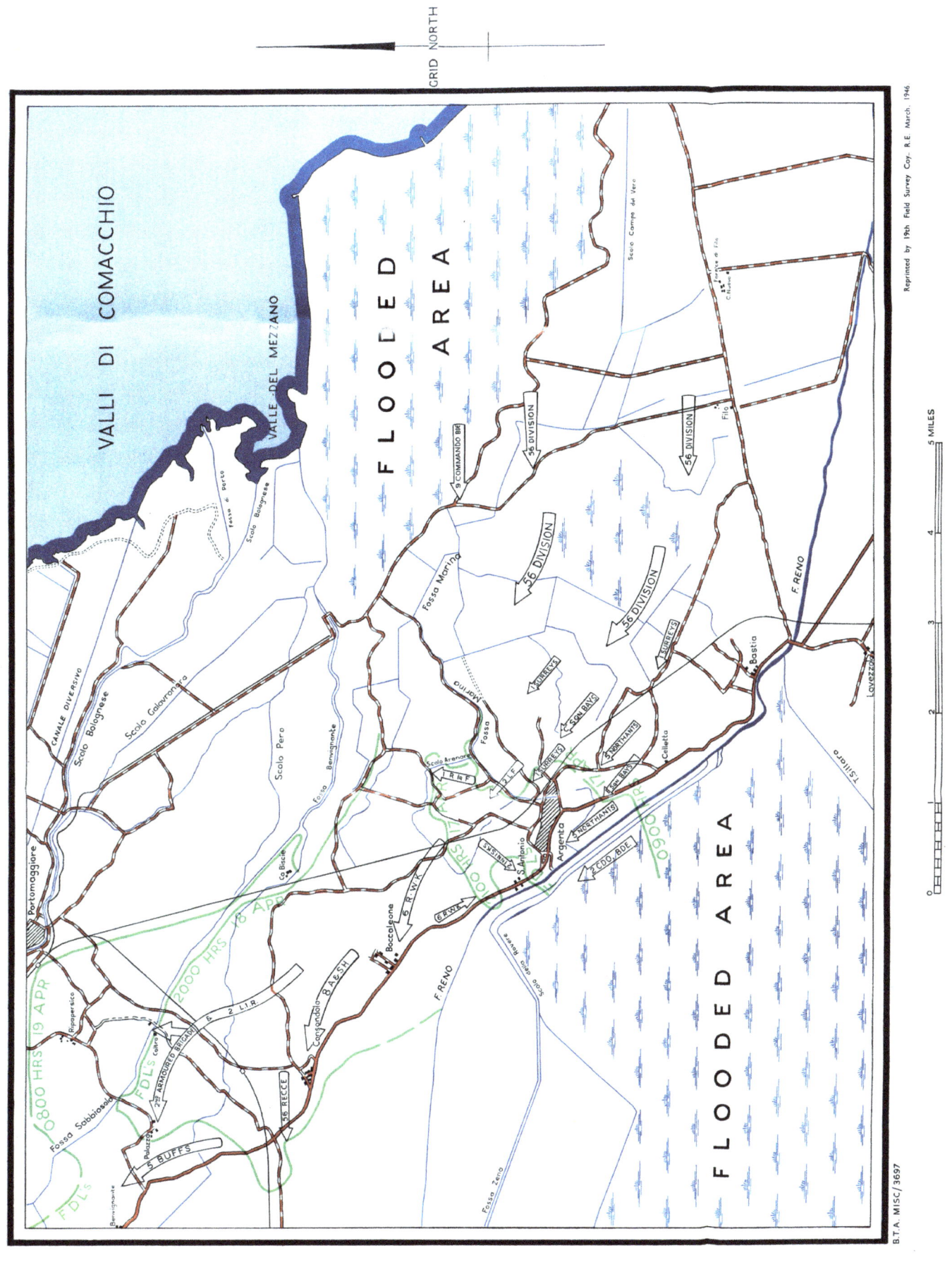

SHOWING ADVANCE 19-23 APR '45

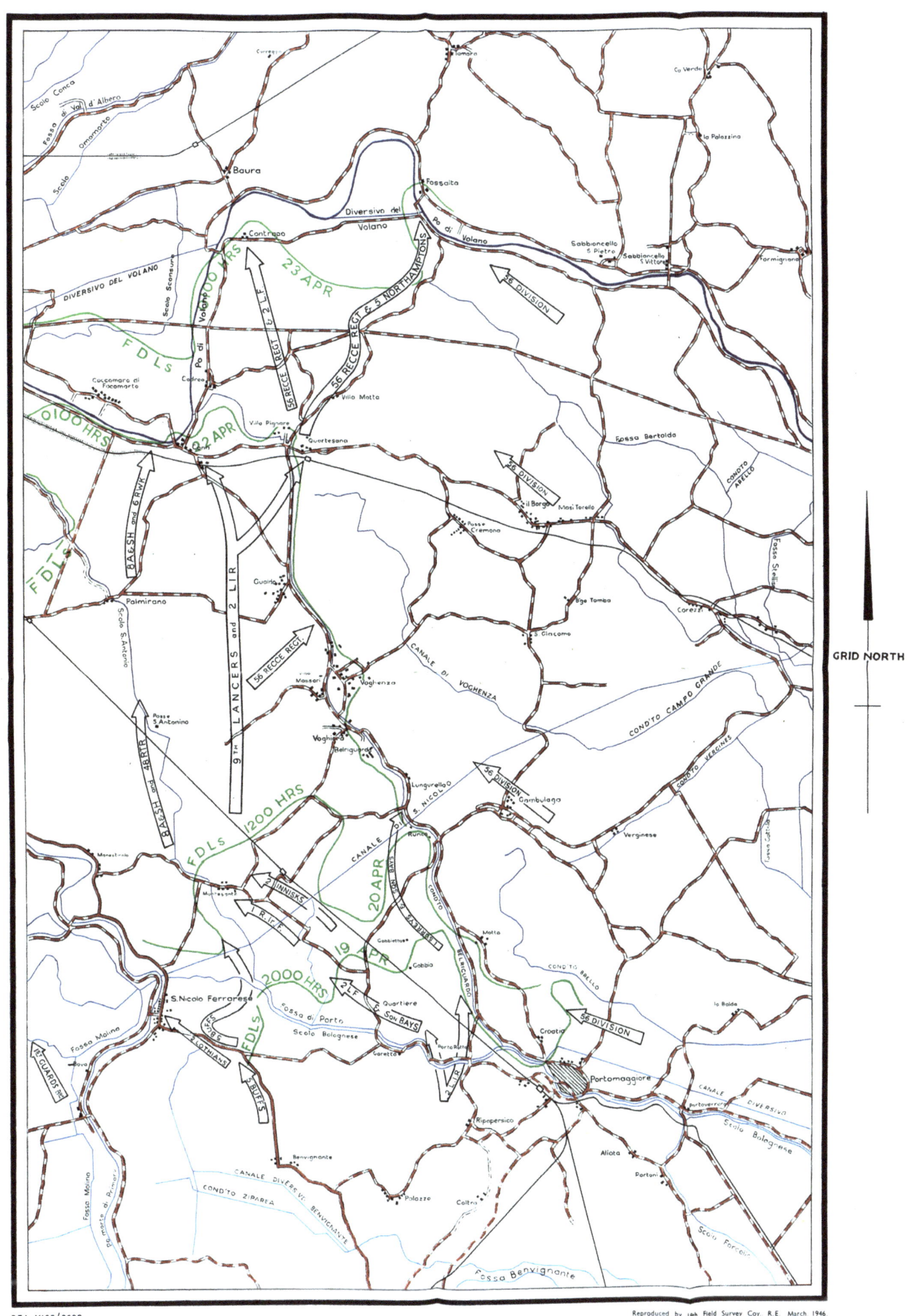

SHOWING ADVANCE 23-25 APR 45

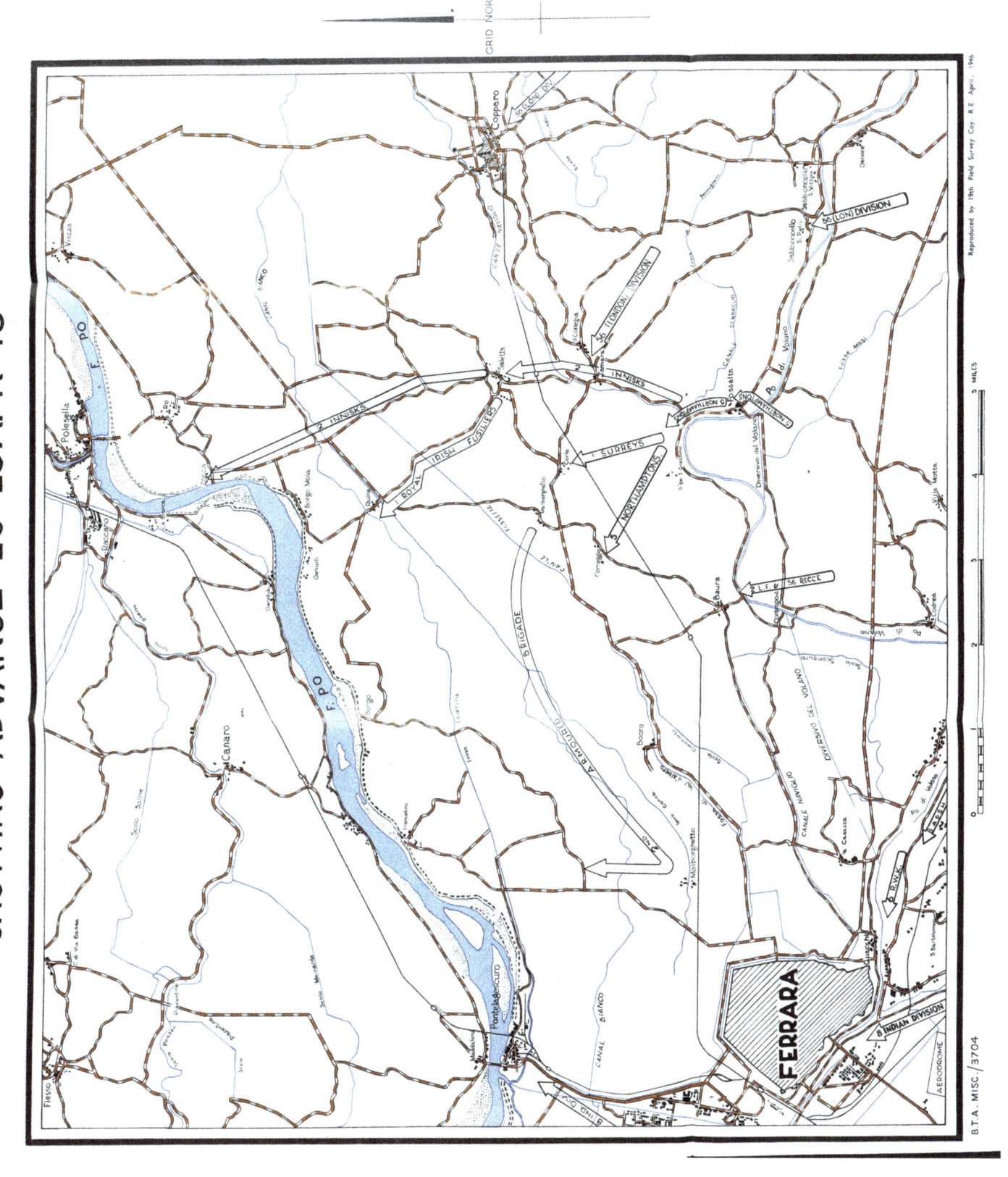

EIGHTH ARMY F.D.Ls AT LAST LIGHT 9 - 25 APR 45.

Main axis of advance 78th Division.

Miles 0 1 2 3 4 5 10 15 20

F.D.L. as at 10th April 1945.

B.T.A. Misc/3707.

Reproduced by 19th Field Survey Coy., R.E. April, 1946.

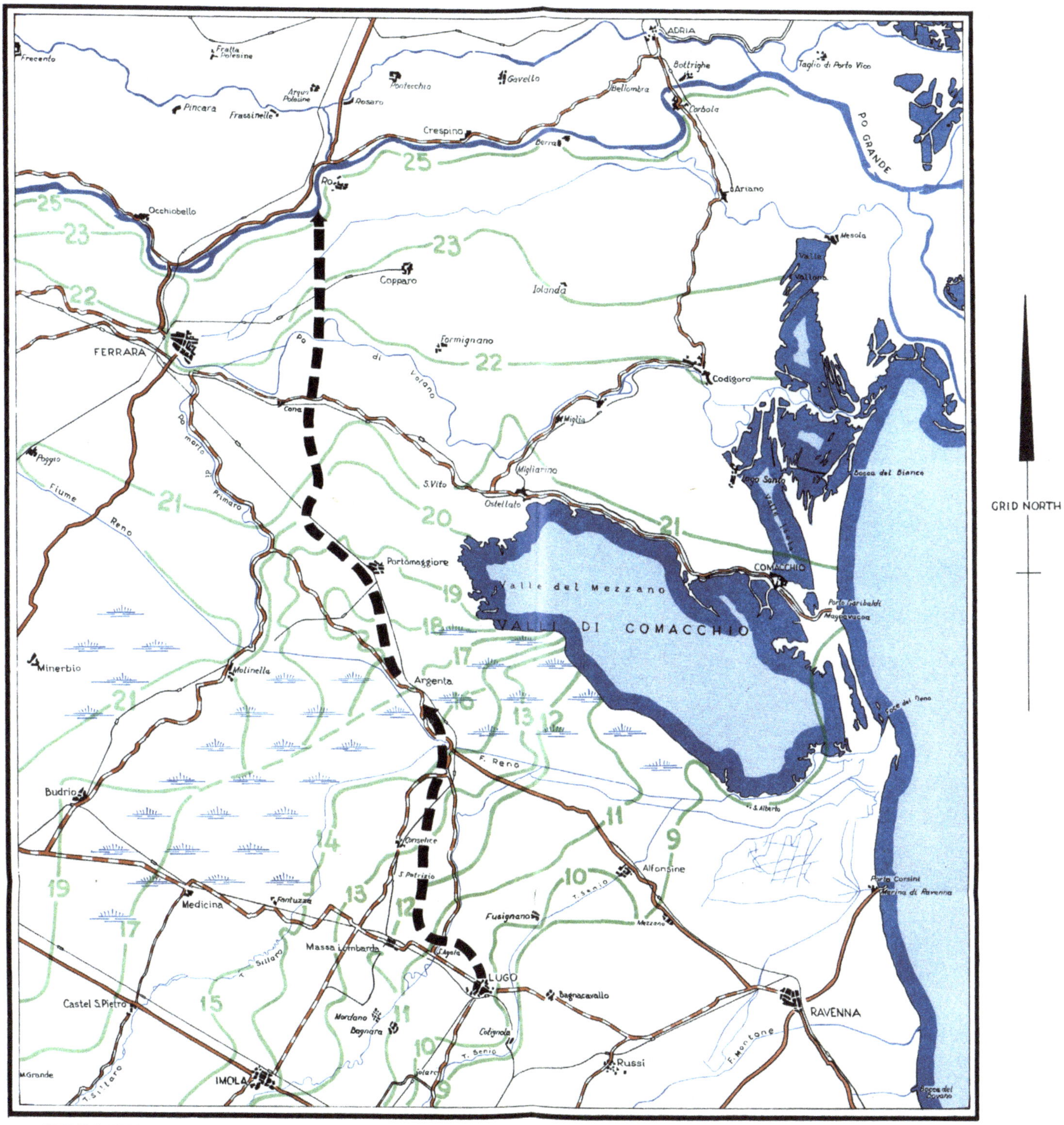

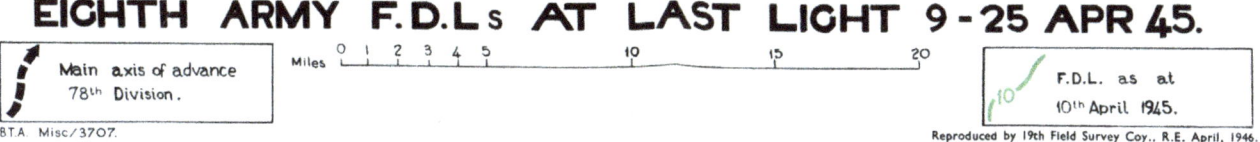

www.ingramcontent.com/pod-product-compliance
Lightning Source LLC
Chambersburg PA
CBHW061056170426
43193CB00025B/2990